HOLT SCIENCE

Skills Workshop

Reading in the Content Area

Teacher's Edition

HOLT, RINEHART AND WINSTON

A Harcourt Classroom Education Company

Austin • New York • Orlando • Atlanta • San Francisco • Boston • Dallas • Toronto • London

AUTHORS

Steven Darian
Rutgers University
Camden, NJ

Stanley Krantz
Cherry Hill High School West
Cherry Hill, NJ

Steven Darian has a Ph.D. in Applied Linguistics from New York University. His research on the language of science has appeared in many scholarly publications. He has been a Fulbright Visiting Professor in India, where he lectured on the language of science.

Stanley Krantz has a M.A. in Science Education from Adelphi University. He has taught middle school and high school science courses for 36 years and has been a science supervisor for 12 years. Stan also teaches science methods at Rutgers University and serves on the executive board of the New Jersey Science Supervisor's Association.

TO THE TEACHER

Our Goals This workbook was designed to help students develop their ability to use those thinking skills that form the building blocks of quantifying and comparing. The Exercises help students integrate these thought modes into their reading, their writing, and their thinking. This workbook is suitable for any student in grades 6-12. It is especially useful for students who are at-risk and students whose first language is not English.

The program can be used in science class to teach individual skills by working through each chapter's Exercises. Using the transparencies, you can build whole lessons for large group skill instruction. Because the chapters are cumulative, the thought patterns introduced early in the sequence are recycled throughout later chapters. Each chapter closes with a glossary, so students can quickly review key concepts from the chapter.

Wherever possible, we've tried to find creative and enjoyable activities to help students learn various thinking skills. We feel strongly that learning the skills taught through these lessons—and applying them—can help raise the scientific abilities of all students. We hope you enjoy the program and that it will help make your teaching a richer and more enjoyable experience.

Teacher's Edition The Teacher's Edition provides suggestions for presenting the material in class, answers to all of the exercises, and a wealth of transparencies for large group instruction. The Exercises make excellent in-class activities, remedial projects, and homework assignments.

Steven Darian
Stan Krantz

Requests for permission to make copies of any part of the work should be mailed to the following address: Permissions Department, Holt, Rinehart and Winston, 10801 N. MoPac Expressway, Austin, Texas 78759.

Printed in the United States of America

ISBN 0-03-064424-0   ISBN 0-03-064423-2

10 11 12 13 14 15   021   06 05 04 03

CONTENTS

Contents, continued

Contents, continued

CHAPTER 7 HYPOTHESIS, PROBABILITY, AND PREDICTION

CHAPTER 8 NUMBERS, WORDS, AND QUANTITIES

Name _____ Date _____ Class _____

1-1 The Importance of Observation and Description

Being able to describe a concept or an image accurately is very important when communicating with someone else. Accurately describing something is not always as easy as it sounds. Have you ever seen something and, several days later, had someone ask you to describe it? Perhaps you have looked at a picture or a drawing in a textbook, and been asked to describe it on a test. How close is your description to the real thing?

In science, it is very important to be able to describe concepts and situations accurately and completely. A scientist must be able to describe his or her experiments and results clearly enough that another scientist can reproduce those findings exactly. Therefore, part of learning science includes developing your ability to describe things as clearly and accurately as possible.

Use Exercise 1 as a game you can play with your classmates. Have each person write a description of your classroom. After you have written your descriptions, compare them. You will probably find differences between each account.

Exercise 1 Observation and Description

Encourage students to work independently until they have completed their classroom descriptions. Then divide them into small groups to compare their responses.

a. Write as complete a description of your classroom as possible.

Answers will vary. Do not expect students to have complete descrip-

tions. The purpose of this exercise is to show students how important

careful observation is and how they probably have not always been

careful observers.

_____

_____

b. List two things that you did not list in your description but were included in a classmate's description.

Make sure students are not discouraged by their omissions. Point out

that it is natural to give an incomplete description.

c. Now list two things that your classmate did not list in his or her description but that you included.

Point out that no one gave a perfectly complete description of the

classroom.

1-2 Spatial Patterns

As an additional exercise, have students choose a vertical object or a horizontal object somewhere in the classroom without revealing their choice. Then, have the students write descriptions for their objects. When the descriptions are written, pair the students and have them try to guess each other's objects.

Try writing a description of your pen or pencil. You could begin by describing the end, or eraser and move down the pen or pencil until you got to the tip. Or you could begin at the tip and describe the object moving upward to the end. Either way, you are depicting each part of the pen or pencil in terms of the part above or below it. You are following a pattern of describing the object along its shaft. This pattern is a **spatial pattern.** The word *spatial* refers to the position of an object or part of an object. Therefore, a *spatial pattern* is a pattern of description that follows the relative positions of the objects or parts of objects.

The spatial pattern that you choose depends on the shape and arrangement of the item you are describing. For example, if you are describing a tall or **vertical** item, such as the office building shown in **Figure 1-1(a),** you would want to start from the bottom and work your way up to the top. Or you might start at the top and work down to the bottom. On the other hand, if you were describing a long, relatively flat, or **horizontal,** subject, such as the bridge shown in **Figure 1-1(b),** you might use a left-to-right or right-to-left pattern.

FIGURE 1-1

(a) Vertical

(b) Horizontal

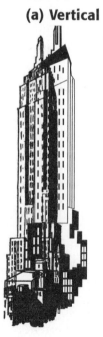
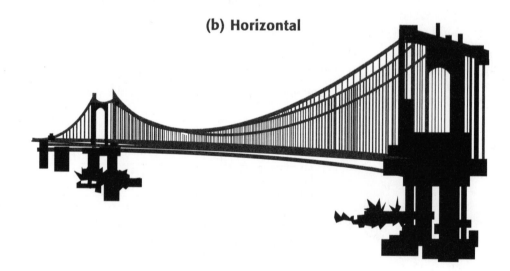

Section 1-2 Spatial Patterns, continued

To describe a circular subject, such as a clock, you might start at the top (the number 12 position of a clock) and continue your description **clockwise.** You could also start at the bottom and continue your description in a **counterclockwise** direction. **Table 1-1** lists several spatial patterns and uses symbols to help illustrate them.

Table 1-1 Spatial Patterns

Pattern	Symbol	Pattern	Symbol
Top-to-bottom	↓	Clockwise	↻
Bottom-to-top	↑	Counterclockwise	↺
Left-to-right	→	In-to-outward	⊚→
Right-to-left	←	Out-to-inward	⊚←

Spatial patterns depend on *spatial relationships*. Remember that the word *spatial* means "position". Spatial relationships describe the position of one item relative to another. **Table 1-2** introduces some terms you are probably familiar with from your math class. These terms are useful for describing spatial relationships.

Table 1-2 Terms for Describing Spatial Relationships

Term	Definition	Example
Perpendicular	being at a 90° angle to another object or line	⊥
Parallel	extending in the same direction, everywhere the same distance apart	‖
Diagonal	at an angle, not 90°, relative to another line or object	◺
Horizontal	flat, parallel to the horizon	—
Vertical	pointing straight upward, perpendicular to the horizon	│

Before students look at Table 1-2, have them review their knowledge of the terms in it. Most students will have seen these terms in previous math courses. Point out that knowledge gained in one school subject can carry over into other subjects.

Section 1-2 Spatial Patterns, continued

A tall, straight tree could be described as **perpendicular** to the ground. You might describe the sugar-phosphate backbones of a DNA strand as being **parallel** to one another and connected by the nucleic-acid bases. As an airplane descends to land, it is **diagonal** to the ground.

Another pattern used to describe things involves numbers and measurements. This pattern is such an important part of science that we will examine the topic in a separate chapter.

Exercise 2 **Spatial Relations**

Complete each of the following tasks:

a. Draw a horizontal line from the point below.

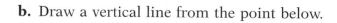

b. Draw a vertical line from the point below.

c. Draw a line that is perpendicular to the line below.

d. Draw a line that is parallel to the line below.

e. Draw a line that is diagonal to the line below and that extends from lower right to upper left.

Section 1-2 Spatial Patterns, continued

Exercise 3 Clockwise and Counterclockwise

Students may have difficulty seeing the motion of wheels represented by still pictures. After students have attempted the exercise, it may be helpful to demonstrate the motion on a small model. A simple model can be made from wheels and elastic bands found at a local hardware store.

Look at the drawings below. Imagine that each set of wheels is connected by cords or rubber bands. As wheel **a** turns in the direction of the arrow, the other wheel(s), also turn. Decide which direction wheel **b** turns. As an example, item 1 is already done for you.

1. **a.** *counterclockwise*

   b. *counterclockwise*

2. **a.** counterclockwise

   b. clockwise

3. **a.** clockwise

   b. clockwise

4. **a.** clockwise

   b. counterclockwise

5. **a.** clockwise

   b. counterclockwise

6. **a.** counterclockwise

   b. clockwise

7. **a.** clockwise

   b. clockwise

8. **a.** counterclockwise

   b. counterclockwise

1.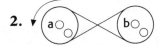

2.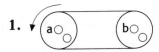

3.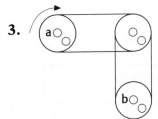

4.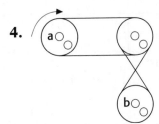

5.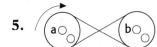

6.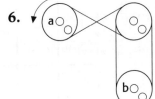

7.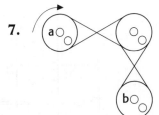

8.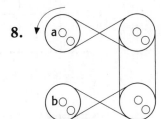

Section 1-2 Spatial Patterns, continued

Exercise 4 **Describing a Three-Dimensional Object**

Complete the following tasks.

a. From the lower left of the grid, count up two boxes and place a dot at that point.

b. Draw a 45° diagonal line running from the first dot toward the upper right. The line should be five boxes long.

c. Draw a dot at the end of the line.

d. From that dot, count over five boxes horizontally to the right and down two boxes vertically. Draw a dot at that point. Connect that dot with the uppermost dot in the center.

e. From the dot on the far right, draw a 45° diagonal line that runs to the lower left. The line should be three boxes long. Draw a dot at the end of the line.

f. At that point, draw a horizontal line that connects the dot to the first dot that you drew. The line should run from right to left.

g. Go back to the previous dot and draw a diagonal line that connects that point to the uppermost point.

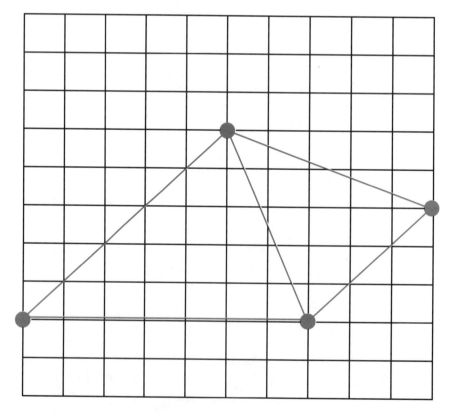

What kind of structure did you draw?

a pyramid _____

CHAPTER

1 OBSERVING AND DESCRIBING

1-3 Using Figurative Language

An accurate description of an object might include a discussion of its size, shape, color, texture, or hardness. To discuss these properties, an author may use **figurative language.** Figurative language often compares two objects that seem very different, but are alike in some important way.

Figure 1-2(a) shows how the shape of two items can be compared. **Figure 1-2(b)** shows how shape can be compared to a letter. **Figure 1-2(c)** shows how shape can be compared to a geometric figure.

Have students practice comparisons by comparing three objects. See how many different yet equally correct comparisons are made for each item.

FIGURE 1-2

(a) The *cone-shaped* flask is called an Erlenmeyer flask.

(b) The *S-shaped* curve in the road produced a dangerous place where drivers needed to slow down.

(c) A *hexagon-shaped,* or six-sided, sign usually means "stop."

Size can also be a basis for comparison. For example, a white dwarf is a *planet-sized* star. You can describe other features of an object by using different combinations of words. The material *amber* could be described as a yellow, *glasslike* pebble. Items can also be compared based on the quality of thickness or thinness. Consider the following description: A *paper-thin* membrane protects the embryo from a hostile environment.

Another way of describing an unknown object is to simply say that it resembles something else. For example, if you needed to describe an eel to a person who has never seen one, you might say that an eel resembles a snake.

Section 1-3 Using Figurative Language, continued

Complete descriptions are formed by combining comparisons of size, shape, and other features. Examine the following three sentences. The first and second sentences are incomplete descriptions of a white dwarf. The third sentence combines the first two to form a more complete description. Exercise 5 gives you practice in combining ideas to complete a description.

(1) A white dwarf is a star.
(2) It is the size of a planet.
(3) A white dwarf is a planet-sized star.

Exercises 6 through 9 will give *you* the chance to describe a variety of things, using all of the techniques you have learned so far.

Exercise 5 **Writing Complete Descriptions**

For each item, combine the first two sentences to form a single sentence. Use the white-dwarf example as a guide.

a. The pyramids are huge buildings.
They are shaped like triangles.

The pyramids are huge, triangle-shaped buildings.

_____

b. The bridge has two supports.
The supports are shaped like pyramids.

The bridge has two pyramid-shaped supports.

_____

c. An igloo is a building.
It is shaped like a dome.

An igloo is a dome-shaped building.

_____

d. Pterodactyls were reptiles that lived 150 million years ago.
They were like birds.

Pterodactyls were birdlike reptiles that lived 150 million years ago.

_____

e. Resin is a thick substance.
It is the color of honey.

Resin is a thick, honey-colored substance.

_____

Section 1-3 Using Figurative Language, continued

Exercise 6   **Using Spatial Relations to Describe Position**

The drawing is available on **Transparency 2.** There is often more than one way of describing the items. Try to elicit as many ways to answer each question as you can.

Study the drawing below and answer the questions that follow it:

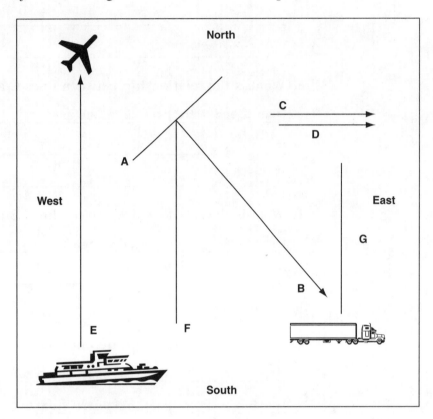

a. Where is the airplane within the box?

The airplane is in the upper left-hand corner of the box.

_____

_____

b. Where is the boat within the box?

The boat is in the lower left-hand corner of the box.

_____

_____

c. What is the location and compass direction of line B?

Line B points downward from the northwest to the southeast. It is

approximately in the center of the drawing.

_____

Section 1-3 Using Figurative Language, continued

d. What is the relationship between lines A and B?

Lines A and B are perpendicular to one another.

_____

_____

e. What is the relationship between lines C and D?

Lines C and D are parallel to one another.

_____

_____

f. What is the relationship between lines B and F?

Lines B and F are diagonal to one another.

_____

_____

g. Describe line E in two different ways.

Line E is a vertical line that points from south to north.

Line E is a vertical line that points from the boat to the plane.

_____

_____

_____

_____

h. What is the relationship between the truck and (i) line G, (ii) line D, (iii) line B?

i. The truck is perpendicular to line G.

_____

ii. The truck is parallel to line D.

_____

iii. Line B is diagonal to the truck.

_____

Section 1-3 Using Figurative Language, continued

Exercise 7 **Using Figurative Language**

The students will probably be familiar with sucrose and sodium chloride but unfamiliar with the other substances. Use this opportunity to point out that they may often be asked to describe unfamiliar things, places, and situations.

Suppose you were asked to describe the following picture to someone who needed to perform an experiment using the equipment shown. Write as complete a description of the image as possible.

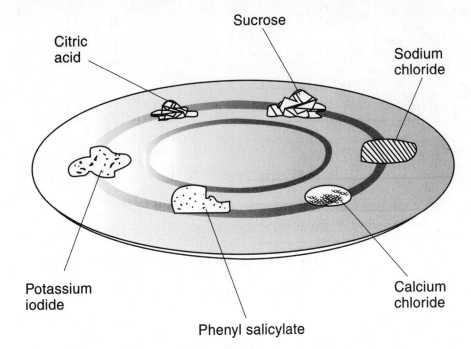

Citric acid

Sucrose

Sodium chloride

Potassium iodide

Phenyl salicylate

Calcium chloride

A round plate contains six small piles of solid material that are equally spaced apart. If the circular dish were a clock face, a small pile of sucrose would be placed at the 1:00 position. Moving around the plate in a clockwise direction, and equally spaced apart are piles of sodium chloride, calcium chloride, phenyl salicylate, potassium iodide, and citric acid.

_____

_____

_____

_____

_____

_____

Section 1-3 Using Figurative Language, continued

Exercise 8   Describing a Model

Describe the model of the following styrene molecule. Styrene is a monomer found in polystyrene. Polystyrene is used to make plastic foam cups and other foam containers.

$$
\begin{array}{ccc}
\text{H} & \text{H} & \\
| & | & \\
\text{C} = \text{C} & - & \text{H}
\end{array}
$$

The letter C has short lines extending vertically above and below it.

Attached to the vertical line above the C is the letter H. Attached to the vertical line below the C is a hexagon. Inside the hexagon is a circle. Two parallel horizontal lines extend from the letter C to the right. Attached to the right of these two lines is another letter C. A vertical line extends above the right-most letter C. Attached to the top of this vertical line is the letter H. A horizontal line extends to the right of the right-most letter C. Attached to the right horizontal line is another letter H.

_____

_____

_____

_____

_____

Section 1-3 Using Figurative Language, continued

Exercise 9 Terms Frequently Used in Descriptions

This exercise is challenging. When reviewing the correct answer with the students, use **Transparency 3.** Use a colored pen to trace the path of the volcanoes on the overhead transparency as students read their responses. This way, students can easily see if they have made a mistake in their description.

Volcanoes are most likely to form at the boundaries of tectonic plates. The solid lines on the map below indicate these boundaries. The dots represent the locations of volcanoes. Study the map below and write out a detailed description of where the volcanoes occur. Begin your description at the southern tip of the South American peninsula. The following terms might be useful in your description:

bends	slopes	arc	continues
branches	tip	coast	runs
descends	semi-circle	turns	north, south, etc...

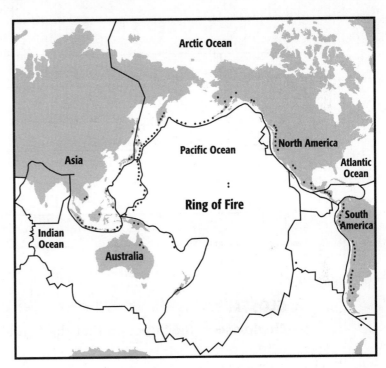

Most of the world's volcanoes occur in an arc called the Ring of Fire, that

follows the edges of tectonic plates. This "ring" begins at the southern

tip of South America. It continues northward along the west coast of

South and Central America. The ring then runs along the western coast of

North America and bends to the west along the southern Alaskan coast.

The path of volcanoes forms an arc that bends toward the south as it

crosses the Pacific Ocean. The ring then slopes downward to the south

west until it reaches about halfway down the eastern coast of Asia. The

Section 1-3 Using Figurative Language, continued

tectonic plate that is a part of the Ring of Fire turns to the southeast

until it is parallel with the southeastern tip of Asia. Then the ring turns

back toward the southwest until it is just north of the midpoint of

Australia. Then the ring forms a semicircle that extends around the east-

ern side of Australia. There are two volcanoes located in the center of

the Ring of Fire. There is also a line of volcanoes that forms a semicircle

around the islands between Asia and Australia.

_____

_____

_____

_____

_____

_____

_____

_____

GLOSSARY

clockwise in the direction that the hands of a clock normally move (3)

counterclockwise in the opposite direction of clockwise (3)

diagonal at an angle, not 90°, relative to another line or object (4)

figurative language words used to equate or find a resemblance between two things that are seemingly different (7)

horizontal flat, parallel to the horizon (2)

parallel extending in the same direction, everywhere the same distance apart, and not meeting (4)

perpendicular being at a 90° angle to another object or line (4)

spatial pattern a pattern of description that follows the relative positions of objects or parts of the objects (2)

vertical pointing straight upward, perpendicular to the horizon (2)

2 DESCRIBING TIME

2-1 Chronological Time

No description of an object or event is complete without placing the object or event in the context of time. For example, if you heard a description of a large mammal with a long trunk and tusks, you would immediately assume that the mammal described was an elephant. However, if you found out that the mammal lived about 10,000 years ago, you might change your mind about the identity of the animal. The animal described was in fact a mammoth, a close relative of today's elephants. Do you see how much difference time can make to an accurate description?

What are some of the ways you use time to organize your life or make sense of the world? Think about it for a moment. Think how different life would be if there were no clocks or watches. This was the case for most of human history. Try to describe what you did yesterday in detail without using any references to the time of day or night. You will find it challenging. Before humans had the concept of the 24-hour day, or the calendar year, events were recalled by relating them to other events that occurred at the same time. For example, Egyptian accounts of events often relate the time of events to the time of the annual flooding of the Nile. Every Egyptian knew when the Nile River flooded in a given year. Therefore, if you told someone that your little brother was born during the last flood, he or she would know exactly when the baby was born.

This method of relative time description only works if the person you are describing the event to knows about your reference. If an Egyptian traveled to China and told a Chinese person that his little brother was born during the last flood, the Chinese person would have no idea when the event occurred.

Now we use a system of years, months, days, hours, minutes, and seconds as a common reference for periods of time. Everyone in the world understands the same reference. Keep in mind that other calendars and methods of time keeping still exist, but the idea of a 24-hour day and a 364- or 365-day year is accepted worldwide.

Time is used in scientific writing in two different ways: *chronological time* and *process time* (a sequence describing a process). **Chronological time** is used for historical events and developments and for things that happen over a period of time. It can be a short period such as hours, days, or weeks. Or it can be a long period such as years, decades, centuries, or billions of years. Read the following passage, which discusses the age of the planet Earth. It has several **specific time markers.** A specific time marker is a word or phrase that contains a date or indicates the passage of time. **Table 2-1** lists some of the possible specific time markers.

Earth's Age

The passage is available on **Transparency 4.** Use the overhead transparency to point out the four specific time markers by underlining or circling them with a colored pen.

The estimated age of Earth, more than 4 billion years, is about 700,000 times as long as the period of recorded history. It is about 50 million times as long as the average human life span. How can we determine what happened so long ago? Scientists have drilled deep into Earth and have examined its many layers to establish a fairly complete picture of its geologic history. Early estimates of Earth's age were made from studying layers of sediment in Earth's crust. The age of Earth could not be estimated accurately, however, until the middle of the twentieth century, when modern methods of establishing the age of materials were developed.

(from Modern Biology)

The above passage contains four specific time markers. Can you locate them? The first three give estimates of the age of Earth: *4 billion years, 700,000 times as long as the period of recorded history,* and *50 million times as long as the average human life span.* The fourth time marker in the passage refers to the time at which the age of Earth could be accurately estimated, *the middle of the twentieth century.* Exercise 1 gives you more practice identifying specific time markers.

Table 2-1 Specific Time Markers

1 hour	60 minutes
1 day	24 hours
1 week	7 days
1 year	365 days 12 months
1 decade	10 years
1 century	100 years
1 millennium	1000 years
the twentieth century	1901–2000
half past noon	12:30 P.M.
new year's eve	December 31

Section 2-1 Chronological Time, continued

Exercise 1   **Time Markers**

a. Read the following passage and pick out the specific time markers that appear. Write the word or phrase of the time marker on the lines provided. The first marker that appears in the passage is written for you on line (i) as an example.

The passage is available on **Transparency 5.** Allow students to work individually. After they have finished, have them help you point out the specific time markers while you underline or circle them on the overhead with a colored pen. You may also wish to point out words that indicate the relative passage of time, such as *next, since, suddenly,* or *abruptly.*

Life Begins

The earliest traces of life are found as tiny fossils in 3.5-billion-year-old rocks from the ancient seas. Earth's first cells were bacteria. Unlike the interior of today's plant and animal cells, the insides of these early forms were like a warehouse—an open space within which all of the contents of a cell were free to move about. For over a billion years, bacteria were the only living things on Earth.

Then, about 1.5 billion years ago, a new kind of organism called the protist, evolved. Most protists are single-celled organisms. The next stage is the appearance of multicellular organisms. The first known fossils of multicellular organisms were found in 630-million-year-old rocks from southern Australia.

All the major groups of organisms that survive today, except plants, originated sometime during the first hundred million years of this period, which is called the Cambrian period. The Cambrian period lasted from just less than 600 million years ago to about 500 million years ago. Life was more diverse in the Cambrian seas than it has ever been since.

In the time span following the Cambrian, a period known as the Ordovician, the seas continued to teem with all forms of living things. The end of the Ordovician period is marked by a drastic change in the fossil record. A large portion of all life-forms suddenly disappeared from Earth, about 440 million years ago. This major mass extinction was the first of five that have occurred during the history of life on Earth.

Another mass extinction of similar magnitude happened abruptly about 360 million years ago. Then, about 100 million years later, the third and greatest of all mass extinctions literally devastated our planet. It happened at the end of what is called the Permian period, about 250 million years ago. At that time, about 96 percent of all

Section 2-1 Chronological Time, continued

animals became extinct. Approximately 35 million years later, a fourth, less devastating mass extinction occurred. Although the specific causes for these events are not clear, evidence suggests that massive geological or climatic changes had come over Earth.

(from Biology: Principles and Explorations)

    i. *3.5-billion-year-old* _____

   ii. For over a billion years _____

_____

  iii. about 1.5 billion years ago _____

_____

  iv. 630-million-year-old _____

_____

   v. sometime during the first hundred million years of this time

period _____

  vi. from just less than 600 million years ago to about 500 million

years ago _____

 vii. about 440 million years ago _____

_____

viii. about 360 million years ago _____

_____

  ix. about 100 million years later _____

_____

   x. about 250 million years ago _____

_____

  xi. Approximately 35 million years later _____

_____

Name_____ Date _____ Class _____

Section 2-1 Chronological Time, continued

Use **Transparency 6** to review the answer to part (b) of Exercise 1. Fill in the answers (or dates) on the lines provided while reviewing the passage.

b. The timeline below indicates periods and events involved in the evolution of organisms on Earth. Using the passage, add approximate dates to the timeline.

Precambrian period	Cambrian period	Ordovician period	Devonian period	Carboniferous period	Permian period	Jurassic period
Earliest traces of life found as tiny fossils	Life on Earth reaches peak of diversity	First mass extinction	Second mass extinction		Third mass extinction	Fourth mass extinction
3.5 billion	600–500	440 million	360 million		250 million	215 million
years ago	million years ago	years ago	years ago		years ago	years ago

Protists evolve

1.5 billion years ago

Copyright © by Holt, Rinehart and Winston. All rights reserved.

READING SKILLS WORKSHEETS **19**

2-2 Process Time

Process time is used to indicate a **sequence.** A sequence is a series of steps leading to some end, result, or conclusion. Read the two sample passages on the following page that use sequences to describe processes. Notice the sequence of events depicted in each passage. The illustrations that accompany the passages will help you visualize the processes described in the text. Many of your science texts will include words, as well as images, to help you learn about scientific processes. You must be able to use both to gain a complete understanding of the topics.

The two passages illustrate two different ways of writing process time. The first passage, "How a Nuclear Power Plant Works," is written as a numerical sequence. Each sentence is numbered, and the events occur in the order of the numbered sequences. The numbers also provide an easy reference to the picture that accompanies the text. Try to follow the steps written in the passage by comparing them to the numbered parts of the image.

FIGURE 2-1 A nuclear power plant generates electricity using a sequence of events.

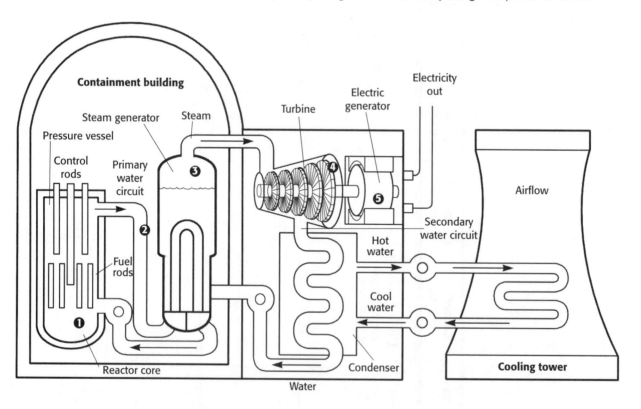

Section 2-2 Process Time, continued

How a Nuclear Power Plant Works

1. Energy released in the reactor core by the nuclear reaction heats the water in the pressure vessel to a very high temperature.
2. The superheated water is pumped from the pressure vessel into the steam generator.
3. The water is then converted into high-pressure steam.
4. After that, the steam is directed against a turbine and causes it to turn.
5. The turbine sets the generator in motion which generates electricity.

(from Holt Environmental Science)

Numbered steps are the easiest way to understand a written sequence. Most sequences you will study will not be written in this obvious way. Read the second passage, "The Water Cycle," and see if you can pick out the sequence of events described.

The Water Cycle

Water is the substance most essential to life. Fortunately, water is not usually destroyed; it just moves from place to place in the process shown in **Figure 2-2** on the next page. In this process, called the water cycle, water moves between the atmosphere and the Earth.

The sun provides the energy that drives the water cycle. Heat from the sun evaporates water from the oceans, from lakes and rivers, from moist soil surfaces, from the leaves of plants, and from the bodies of other organisms. As water vapor rises, it cools and expands. As it cools, it condenses and forms tiny droplets of water in the clouds. When the clouds touch the cold air, the droplets are released as rain, sleet, or snow. Because oceans cover most of the planet, most precipitation falls on the oceans.

The precipitation that falls on land may just evaporate again into the atmosphere. Or it may collect in streams and rivers that flow into oceans. Or the precipitation may soak into the soil. Water that soaks into the soil may be used immediately by plants, or it may seep down through the soil and rocks until it reaches a layer of rock and clay, called ground water. Then the process begins again and continues until the end of time.

(from Holt Environmental Science)

The passage "The Water Cycle" appears on **Transparency 7.** As you review the numbered list of events generated from this passage, use a colored pen to insert numbers at the corresponding sentences in the passage on the overhead. Doing so will help the students link the numbered list to the sequence described in the passage.

Section 2-2 Process Time, continued

FIGURE 2-2 The Water Cycle

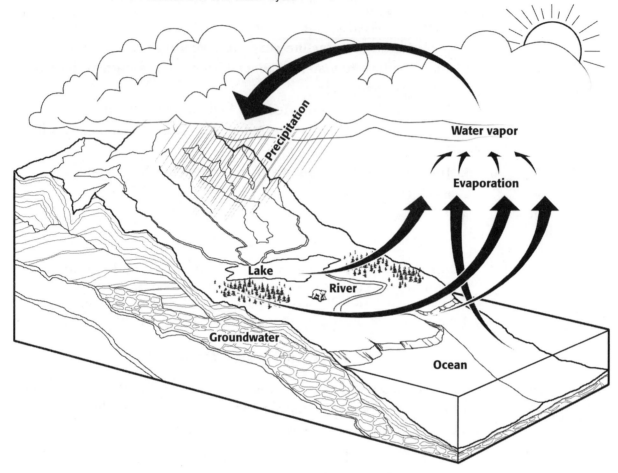

In order to fully understand the passage, you might want to break it up into a numbered list of events in chronological order. Any sequential passage can be turned into a numbered list of events resembling the first passage on how a nuclear power plant works. The following is an example of how the water-cycle passage might break down into a numbered list:

1. The sun heats water in oceans, lakes, rivers, moist soil, leaves of plants, and bodies of other organisms.
2. The water vapor rises in the atmosphere.
3. It cools and expands.
4. The water vapor condenses and forms tiny droplets in the clouds.
5. When the clouds contact cold air, the water falls to Earth as rain, sleet, or snow.
6. Water collects in oceans, streams, rivers, or ground water.
7. The cycle begins again.

Exercise 2 gives you the opportunity to practice breaking down a written passage into a chronological list of events.

Section 2-2 Process Time, continued

Some students may not be familiar with the technique of making flowcharts. If students need help with this technique, have them try to make a simple flowchart of what they do in the morning to get ready to leave their home. This familiar subject should make it easy for students to focus on how a flowchart works.

Notice in the passage on the water cycle that some of the steps in the sequence occur at the same time, or **simultaneously.** For example, the sun evaporates water from many sources at the same time. It can be difficult to envision steps occurring simultaneously. Making a diagram, such as a flowchart, can help you get all of the necessary information out of a complicated passage. **Figure 2-3** is an example of a flowchart that could be used to help clarify the information in the water-cycle passage. Exercise 3 allows you to practice turning a written sequence of events into a flowchart.

FIGURE 2-3 Flowcharts allow you to diagram events that happen simultaneously.

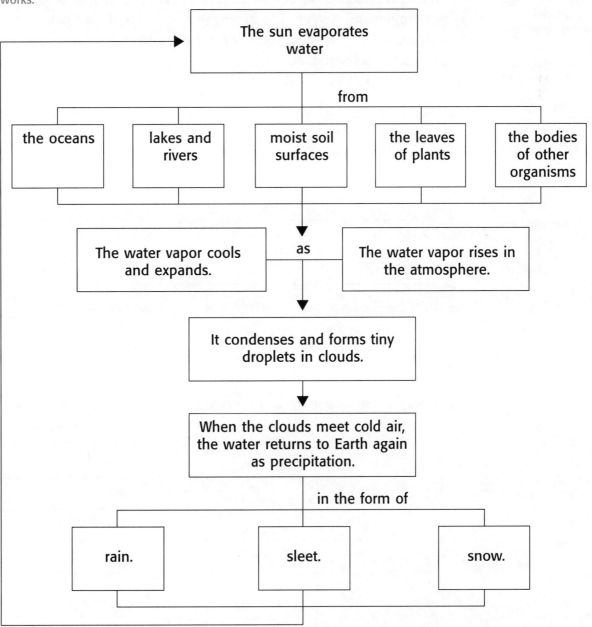

Section 2-2 Process Time, continued

Exercise 2 **Chronological Lists**

The following, which requires a supply of toys used to build objects, such as Legos™ or Tinkertoys™, can be used as an additional exercise.

1. Divide the class into an even number of small groups (three to five students in each group).

2. Each group should build an object of its members choosing.

3. Have each group write detailed instructions for building the chosen object. The instructions can be written using any of the methods for describing process time given in this section.

4. Have groups exchange instructions and assemble their new piece by following each other's instructions.

5. Have each group tell how easy, or difficult, the instructions were to follow.

Read the following passage and make a numerical list of the steps involved in the described process.

What Happens During Photosynthesis

Plant cells have organelles called chloroplasts. Chloroplasts contain chlorophyll, a green pigment. Chlorophyll absorbs most of the colors in sunlight, but not green. Plants look green because chlorophyll reflects green light.

The light energy absorbed by chlorophyll is used to split water into hydrogen and oxygen. The hydrogen is then combined with carbon dioxide from the air surrounding the plant to make sugar. Oxygen is given off as a byproduct.

(from Holt Science & Technology: Life Science)

1. Chlorophyll absorbs light energy.

_____

_____

2. Light energy splits water into hydrogen and oxygen.

_____

_____

3. Hydrogen combines with carbon dioxide from the air.

_____

_____

4. Hydogen and carbon dioxide make sugar.

_____

_____

5. Oxygen is given off as a byproduct.

_____

_____

Section 2-2 Process Time, continued

Exercise 3   Simultaneous Events in a Process

Students may still have difficulty with the idea of events happening simultaneously. In the passage "Where Elements Come From" point out the words that denote simultaneous events. These words include *as* and *but also*.

Read the following passage and use page 26 to make a flowchart diagramming the events described in the text.

Where the Elements Come From

According to current theory, sometime between 12 billion and 16 billion years ago, the entire universe could fit on a pinhead. Then with unbelievable violence, the universe exploded, an event scientists named the big bang. Immediately after the big bang, temperatures were in the millions of kelvins. The temperatures were so high that matter could not exist, only energy could exist. As the universe expanded, it cooled. When the universe cooled to a few thousand kelvins, some of its energy was converted to matter in the form of electrons, protons, and neutrons. As the universe continued to cool, these particles formed the first atoms, almost all hydrogen but also some helium.

Over time, huge clouds of hydrogen accumulated. Gravitational attraction pulled the clumps of hydrogen closer and closer together. As the clouds became denser, pressures and temperatures at the centers of the hydrogen clouds increased and stars were born. In the high-temperature centers of stars, nuclear reactions took place. A nuclear reaction is a reaction involving protons and neutrons in the nuclei of atoms. In the nuclear reactions in the centers of the first stars, hydrogen nuclei fused with one another to form helium nuclei.

(from Holt Chemistry Visualizing Matter)

Section 2-2 Process Time, continued

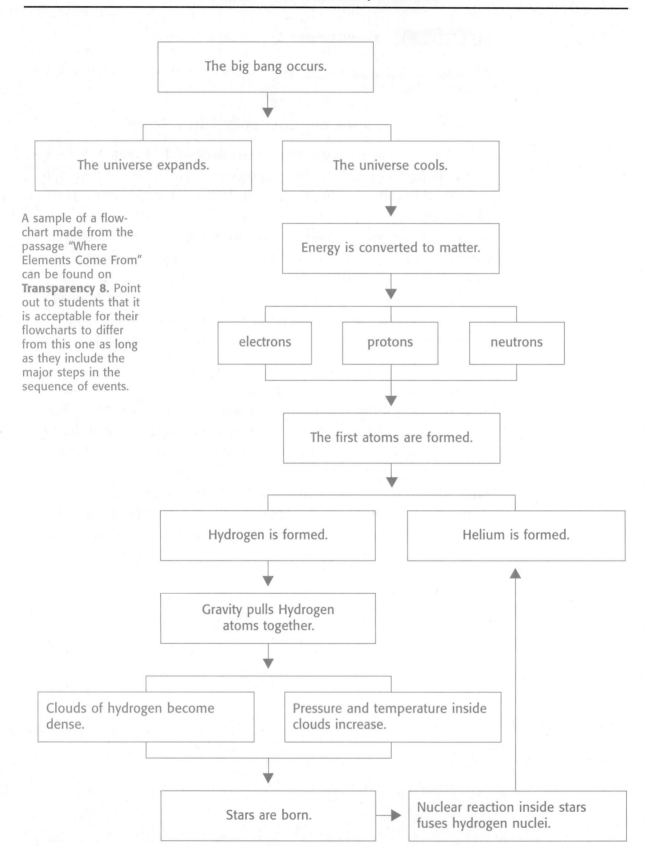

A sample of a flow-chart made from the passage "Where Elements Come From" can be found on **Transparency 8.** Point out to students that it is acceptable for their flowcharts to differ from this one as long as they include the major steps in the sequence of events.

The big bang occurs.

The universe expands.

The universe cools.

Energy is converted to matter.

electrons

protons

neutrons

The first atoms are formed.

Hydrogen is formed.

Helium is formed.

Gravity pulls Hydrogen atoms together.

Clouds of hydrogen become dense.

Pressure and temperature inside clouds increase.

Stars are born.

Nuclear reaction inside stars fuses hydrogen nuclei.

CHAPTER

2   DESCRIBING TIME

2-3 General Time Markers

This passage can be found on **Transparency 9.** Before students have a chance to look at Table 2-2, ask them to point out words that they think are general time markers in the passage. Circle them on the overhead using a colored marker.

The following passage describes how the solar system formed.

Formation of the Solar System

About 4 billion to 5 billion years ago, shock waves from a supernova (a giant exploding star) or some other force caused a cloud of dust and gas to contract. The cloud of dust and gas that formed our solar system over time is called the solar nebula. When the temperature at the center of the nebula became hot enough, hydrogen fusion began and the sun was formed. About 99 percent of the matter in the solar nebula became part of the sun.

During a period of roughly 100 million years, the small bodies of matter in the solar nebula came together to form what are called planetesimals. Through collisions and the force of gravity, some of these planetesimals gradually joined to form much larger bodies called protoplanets. Eventually, the protoplanets condensed into our existing moons and planets.

(from Modern Earth Science)

Even though specific time markers come in the first sentences of each paragraph, you understand the sequence of events because the author uses many **general time markers.** These relate the time of one event to the time of another event. For example, you know that hydrogen fusion occurs after the temperature at the center of the nebula reaches a certain point. The author uses the word *when* to indicate the time at which hydrogen fusion occurs. *When* is a general time marker.

As an additional exercise, ask students to come up with other ways to write a passage in which a sequence of events is described. Students might think of writing a list of events and labeling each event with the date or time of day to put the events in chronological order.

Table 2-2, on page 28, lists several different time relationships and lists some words and phrases that are used to indicate those relationships. **Section 2-2** dealt with sequences used to describe processes. You saw two different ways to include process time in a text: as a chronological list or as written text. In a chronological list, the numbers become time markers. These numbers can be cardinals (1, 2, 3, etc.), as they were in the first passage of **Section 2-2,** or ordinals, as shown in the short passage below.

The Scientific Method

First, ask a question. Second, form a hypothesis. Third, test the hypothesis. Fourth, analyze the results. Fifth, draw conclusions. Sixth, communicate the results.

(from Holt Science and Technology: Physical Science)

Section 2-3 General Time Markers, continued

Table 2-2 General Time Markers

Words used at the beginning of an event	Words used in a sequence	Words used for things that happened before other things	Words used for things that are happening simultaneously	Words used to indicate the end of an event
First	after that	before	as	finally
At first	as soon as	but first	at the same time	at last
In the first place	first, second, etc.	by the time	during	the final
To begin with	next	prior to	while	last
To start	then		meanwhile	
At the beginning	when			
In the beginning	following that			
	subsequently			
	eventually			
	once			

There are other ways to present a sequence of events, steps, or activities. A chronological list can also be made using the letters of the alphabet instead of numbers. Time markers, such as *first, next,* and *then,* can put events in order. See Table 2-2 for more examples of time markers that can indicate a sequence. Maybe you can think of even more ways to write a passage in which a sequence of events is described.

Exercise 4   **Time and Sequence Words**

Read the following passage, and list the sentences or phrases containing time markers used to describe the sequence of events.

> Point out words and phrases that indicate a sequence, including *at first, when,* and *then.* Also point out words that indicate duration of time, such as *billions of years.* Finally, point out other time markers, such as *now.*

Cycles of the Universe

We saw earlier how our sun, moon, and planets came into being. But that stage is only the first stage in the life of a star. The second stage is the one our solar system is in now. This second stage lasts as long as the star, in our case the sun, has enough energy, or enough hydrogen, to keep it burning.

Section 2-3 General Time Markers, continued

When hydrogen begins to run out, the star enters the third stage. At first, the star contracts; then it swells to enormous size. Some stars become giants, while others become supergiants. Giants are 10 or more times bigger than the sun. Supergiants are at least 100 times bigger than the sun.

When its atomic energy is completely gone, a star enters its final stage of evolution. Gravity causes the last of the matter in the star to collapse inward. What is left is a hot, dense core of matter called a white dwarf. White dwarfs shine for billions of years before they cool completely.

Some white dwarfs simply cool and die. During the process of cooling, others create one or more large explosions. A white dwarf that has such an explosion is called a nova. If the star was a supergiant, the white dwarf becomes a supernova after its huge explosion.

After exploding, some supernovas contract into a tiny, incredibly dense ball of neutrons, called a neutron star. A spoonful of matter from a neutron star would weigh 100 million tons on Earth. The remains of other massive stars contract with such a force that they crush their dense core and leave what astronomers think is a hole in space, or a black hole. The gravity of a black hole is so great that not even light can escape from it.

(from Modern Earth Science)

a. But that stage is only the first stage in the life of a star. _____

_____

_____

b. The second stage is the one our solar system is in now. _____

_____

_____

c. This second stage lasts as long as the star, in our case the sun, has

enough energy, or enough hydrogen, to keep it burning. _____

_____

Section 2-3 General Time Markers, continued

d. When hydrogen begins to run out, the star enters the third stage. _____

_____

_____

e. At first, the star contracts; _____

_____

_____

f. then it swells to enormous size _____

_____

_____

g. Some stars become giants, while others become supergiants. _____

_____

_____

h. When its atomic energy is completely gone, a star enters its final

stage of evolution. _____

_____

i. White dwarfs shine for billions of years before they cool completely. ____

_____

_____

j. During the process of cooling, others create one or more large

explosions. _____

_____

k. After exploding, some supernovas contract into a tiny, incredibly

dense ball of neutrons, called a neutron star. _____

_____

Name_____ Date _____ Class _____

Exercise 5 **Recalling Time Sequences**

This exercise requires students to recall the events in the passage "Formation of the Solar System," found on page 27. If students have difficulty recalling the events in order, have them re-read the passage. Then try the exercise again. This exercise could also be completed by copying the sentences on a piece of paper, cutting them into strips, and manipulating them to put them physically in the correct chronological order. **Transparency 9** can be used to review the answers to the exercise.

It is important not only to be able to read a passage and understand any time sequences described, but also retain the information in its correct chronological order. Without looking back through the chapter, number the sentences below in their proper chronological sequence. A few of the steps are already numbered for you. You must fill in the numbers for the rest.

__10__ The moons and planets come into being.

__4__ Hydrogen fusion begins.

__1__ Shock waves from a supernova cause a cloud of dust and gas to contract.

__6__ Small bodies of matter in the solar nebula come together.

__5__ The sun is formed.

__2__ The cloud of dust and gas form a solar system in the solar nebula.

__8__ Planetesimals join together through collisions and gravity.

__9__ Protoplanets are formed.

__3__ The temperature at the center of the nebula becomes very hot.

__7__ Planetesimals are formed.

Exercise 6 **Fill In the Time Markers**

This passage, with its blank lines, can be found on **Transparency 10.** After the students have had a chance to complete the exercise, ask them to help you fill in the blanks on the overhead. You may want to make a few transparencies of this passage so that you may fill in the blanks with more than one set of time markers. This way, you can show the students that there are many different ways to convey the same idea.

Fill in the blank spaces in the passage below with appropriate time markers. If you need help, check back over the list of time markers in Table 2-2. Use as many different time markers as possible. The figure following the passage may help you establish the correct sequence of events.

Formation of a Coral Reef

Corals are small marine animals that live in warm, shallow sea water. _____First_____, a coral extracts minerals from the ocean water and uses them to build a hard outer skeleton.

_____Second_____, corals attach to each other to form large colonies. _____After that_____, new corals grow on top of dead ones and form a coral reef, which is a submerged ridge made up of millions of coral skeletons.

Section 2-3 General Time Markers, continued

Some coral reefs form around tropical volcanic islands. The coral colony grows in the shallow water near the shore. This type of coral reef around the coast of an island is called a fringing reef.

_____When_____ the ocean floor bends under the weight of the volcano, both the volcano and the reef sink.

_____Then_____, the coral reef builds higher because the animals can live only near the surface of the water. The coral reef thus forms a barrier reef offshore around the remnant of the volcanic island. _____Eventually_____, the island disappears completely under water, leaving a nearly circular coral reef, called an atoll, surrounding a shallow lagoon.

(from Modern Earth Science)

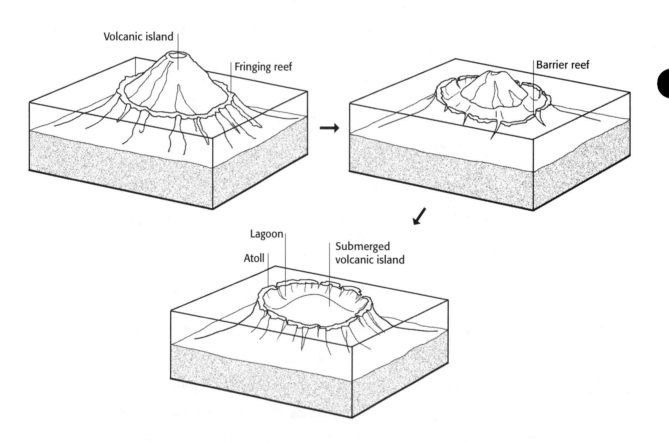

Section 2-3 General Time Markers, continued

Exercise 7   **Using Time Markers**

Using at least five of the time markers from Table 2-2, write a paragraph describing what you did last weekend

Answers will vary. Make sure students have included at least five of the

words from Table 2-2.

_____

_____

_____

_____

_____

_____

_____

_____

_____

_____

_____

_____

_____

_____

_____

_____

_____

2-4 Marked and Unmarked Patterns

Patterns indicating time relationships can be marked or unmarked. A **marked pattern** has a word or phrase to indicate the relationship. The passages you have read so far include specific or general time markers. The time markers *mark* the time patterns. **Unmarked patterns** do not have words or phrases to indicate the time relationship. For this reason, unmarked patterns are sometimes harder to detect and understand.

In the language of science, a marked pattern may be called **explicit:** it is stated specifically in writing or in speaking. An unmarked pattern is **implicit:** it is not stated but is **implied.** The reader has to infer, or guess, the time pattern or the relationship from the nature of the material. The following passage on how nerve impulses travel gives examples of both marked and unmarked relationships.

The Journey of a Nerve Impulse

The passage "The Journey of a Nerve Impulse" can be found on **Transparency 11.** Use the overhead to have students help you circle all of the time markers in this passage. Point out that phrases containing time markers denote *marked* relationships. Then, with the students' help, underline any *unmarked* phrases.

A nerve impulse can travel only so far before it reaches the end of the axon. In most cases, neurons do not touch each other directly. They are separated by a tiny gap called a synapse.
[1] When a nerve impulse reaches the end of an axon, it must cross the synapse if the message is to continue. In most cases, a message is unable to "jump" from one neuron to another. Instead, the impulse is carried across the synapse by chemical messengers called neurotransmitters. When a nerve impulse reaches the end of the axon, neurotransmitters are emptied into the synapse. [2] The neurotransmitters diffuse across the synapse and bind to receptors in the membrane of the adjacent neuron.

(from Holt Biology Visualizing Life)

The sentence numbered (1) is a *marked* sentence. The time marker *when* explicitly states a time pattern. The sentence numbered (2) is *unmarked*. There is no time marker in sentence (2). You can assume that after the neurotransmitter is emptied into the synapse, it diffuses across the synapse to deliver the message or impulse, but this time relationship is implicit, or implied. Exercise 8 gives you additional practice in spotting marked and unmarked relationships.

Section 2-4 Marked and Unmarked Patterns, continued

Exercise 8 **Marked or Unmarked?**

Read the following passage and decide whether the numbered sentences are marked or unmarked. Write "marked" or "unmarked" next to the corresponding numbers on the lines provided. Then on the next line write the marker if there is one.

Solid as a Rock

You all know the phrase *solid as a rock.* Well, that phrase may be true for human time. But for geological time, rocks aren't solid at all. Or rather we can say that rocks change over time. There are three kinds of rocks: *igneous, sedimentary,* and *metamorphic.* Any of the three types of rock can be changed into another type. Various geological forces and processes cause rock to change from one type to another and back again. This series of changes is called the rock cycle.

[1] The process begins with the eruption of volcanoes and the cooling of magma. Magma is hot, molten rock, from the earth's interior. It is the parent material for all rocks. Magma is called lava if it cools at Earth's surface. [2] Magma that eventually cools and hardens forms igneous rock. [3] Once a body of igneous rock has formed, forces such as wind and waves break the rock into small fragments. Rocks, minerals, and organic matter that have been broken into fragments are known as sediment. [4] When the sediment deposits harden after being compressed and cemented together, they form sedimentary rocks.

[5] If the new sedimentary rocks are subject to tremendous pressure, extreme heat, and chemical processes, they can be changed into a third type of rock, called metamorphic rock. [6] If that heat and pressure become even more intense, the metamorphic rock will melt and form magma. [7] This magma may then cool and form new rock. What kind of rock—igneous, sedimentary, or metamorphic—will this new rock be?

(from Modern Earth Science)

1. marked
   _____
   begins
   _____

2. marked
   _____
   eventually
   _____

Section 2-4 Marked and Unmarked Patterns, continued

3. marked _____

   once _____

4. marked _____

   when _____

5. unmarked _____

   _____

6. unmarked _____

   _____

7. marked _____

   then _____

GLOSSARY

chronological time time that involves specific dates and times, for example, 1600 B.C.E or 8 A.M. (15)

explicit stated or indicated directly (34)

general time marker a word or phrase that indicates a time relationship (27)

implicit not stated but implied (34)

implied suggested but not stated directly (34)

marked pattern a time pattern that is indicated (or marked) by a time word or phrase (34)

process time time relationships that indicate a sequence (20)

sequence a series of steps leading to some end or result (20)

simultaneously existing or occurring at the same time (23)

specific time marker a word or phrase that contains a date or indicates the passage of time (15)

unmarked pattern a pattern whose meaning is not stated directly but is implied (34)

CHAPTER

 3 **DEFINITIONS**

3-1 Parts of a Definition

To begin this lesson, point out that it is not easy to fully define things, even the simplest things. For example, ask students to define the term *table.* Some common definitions might be: "It has four legs." "It's a flat surface." Point out that tables can have one, two, or three legs or no legs at all. And point out that a bench or a stool can also be a flat surface with four legs. Students should be aware that none of the above responses are a complete definition. A complete definition would distinguish a table from all other objects.

Can you imagine trying to read a science textbook in which none of the scientific terms were defined? It would be like trying to read material in a foreign language. The world of science has its own language. If you do not know what the words mean, you will never be able to understand the concepts that result from scientific discoveries.

You cannot really understand something unless you are able to define it. Many scientific terms are easy to define when you realize where the term originated. One way to create a new word is to combine old, familiar words to form new ideas. For example, take the word *aerospace. Aero* refers to the atmosphere that surrounds Earth. You might not recognize by looking at the word that *aero* relates to the air, but saying the word out loud helps you make the connection. *Aero* sounds like the word *air. Space* refers to the region beyond Earth's atmosphere. Until recently, the two regions were very different. But with the development of rockets, they became part of one concept. As a result, the United States Air Force invented the term *aerospace.* Can you think of some other words that were created in the same way?

The study of the origins of words is called **etymology.** Just as the origin of the word *aerospace* made the definition clear, knowing where a word comes from can be a useful tool in determining a definition. But how do you define a word whose meaning is not obvious in its origin? Your first instinct is probably to look the word up in a dictionary or glossary. Dictionaries contain **formal definitions** for many words. A formal definition consists of several parts: a *term,* a *class word,* and one or more *limiting features.* We will examine each of these three parts separately.

Term

The **term** is the word that is being defined. Often a term is defined within the text itself. You will frequently see sentences like the following: *A chemical is a substance with a definite composition.* In this sentence, *chemical* is obviously the term being defined. Sometimes a term will be introduced in a sentence, but a definition will not be given. In these cases, you might need to look the term up in a dictionary or in the glossary in the back of your textbook.

Exercise 1   **Dissecting Terms**

The terms on the following page were created by combining two simpler words. Give the meanings of each part of the term, then try to deduce the meaning of the whole term. Note that some terms contain more than one separate word.

Section 3-1 Parts of a Definition, continued

As an additional exercise, have students figure out the meanings for other terms that are formed by combining two simpler terms. Some examples might include *radiotelescope*, *space-time*, *geophysics*, or *biochemistry*.

a. nuclear fusion

nuclear   having to do with the nucleus of an atom

fusion   the combining, or fusing of things together

nuclear fusion   the combining of two nuclei to form a larger nucleus

b. biodegradable

bio   having to do with living things

degradable   able to be broken down into parts

biodegradable   capable of being broken down by living things in the environment

c. hydroelectricity

hydro   having to do with water

electricity   energy from moving electrons

hydroelectricity   energy from moving electrons that was created by falling water

d. exoskeleton

exo   outside

skeleton   supportive structure

exoskeleton   an external support system

e. activation energy

activation   the act of starting a reaction

energy   the ability to do work

activation energy   the energy needed to begin a reaction

Section 3-1 Parts of a Definition, continued

Class Word

Make sure students understand that Table 3-1 is not an all-inclusive list of class words. It is only a set of examples. Have students brainstorm lists of general and specific class words. Make a table similar to Table 3-1 on the board using the words generated by the students. Then, have the students find at least one term belonging to each class.

Once you have determined what term you wish to define, you must determine the general category to which the term belongs. The category (or class) to which a term belongs is called a **class word.** A class word is like a family: it has several members. Take the following sentence for example: *A hammer is a tool.* A hammer is certainly not the only type of tool. Saws, drills, and screwdrivers are also tools. The word *tool* indicates the family to which all of these items belong.

A class word does not always complete a definition. For example, read the following sentence:

Astronomy is a science.

Yes, the sentence tells you something about the definition of the term *astronomy*, but it does not tell you much. The word *science* is a general class word. There are three different types of class words: *general, specific,* and *repetitive*. How do you know if a class word is general, specific, or repetitive?

A **general class word** represents something that is hard to visualize, such as *device, method,* or *process*. A **specific class word** represents something much more tangible. To decide whether a class word is specific or general, close your eyes and try to get a mental picture of what the word represents. It is much easier to close your eyes and picture a tool, an animal, or a kind of fruit than it is to picture science or a process. **Table 3-1** lists some general and specific class words.

Table 3-1 General and Specific Class Words

General class words		Specific class words	
structure	device	metal	instrument
substance	method	machine	fruit
concept	science	tool	animal
policy	process	furniture	container

Point out that for truly unfamiliar terms, it is best not to use repetitive class words. If a term is completely foreign to students, the repetitive class word is not likely to add to their understanding. In other words, it is often a bad idea to use a term in its own definition.

In some cases, the class word may be the same as the term, or part of the term, being defined. This type of device is called a **repetitive class word.** Look back at Exercise 1. This exercise showed you how to break a complicated term into understandable parts. Each of these terms could be defined using a repetitive class word because each part of the term is a word that the reader is likely to understand. For instance, *hydroelectricity* can be defined as electricity made by falling water.

Section 3-1 Parts of a Definition, continued

The following sentence gives you another example of a definition in which a repetitive class word is acceptable: *Acid rain is a form of rain that results from certain chemicals in the air. Acid rain* is the term to be defined. *Rain* is part of the term, but it is also part of the definition. Therefore, *rain* is a repetitive class word.

If a class word is going to be helpful, it must be more familiar to the reader than the term that is being defined. On the other hand, it should not be too general. For this reason, you should avoid using class words like *thing, something,* or *object.* These words do not increase understanding. A good rule of thumb is to use the most specific class word that you can.

Exercise 2   **Class Words**

Encourage students to use class words other than those listed.

Choose a class word for the topics below. If you need help thinking of class words, you can choose from the following list.

a metal	an organ	a condition
a person	a field	a process
an instrument	a science	an animal
a tool		

a. Copper is _a metal_____.

b. A drill is _a tool_____.

c. Chemistry is _a science_____.

d. Aerospace is _a field_____.

e. A computer is _an instrument_____.

f. An engineer is _a person_____.

g. A carnivore is _an animal_____.

h. Drought is _a condition_____.

i. Photosynthesis is _a process_____.

j. The heart is _an organ_____.

Section 3-1 Parts of a Definition, continued

Exercise 3   **General or Specific**

For each of the sentences in Exercise 2, decide whether the class word is general or specific.

a. <u>specific</u>   f. <u>specific</u>

b. <u>specific</u>   g. <u>specific</u>

c. <u>general</u>   h. <u>general</u>

d. <u>general</u>   i. <u>general</u>

e. <u>general</u>   j. <u>specific</u>

Limiting Features

Once you have a class word do you have a complete definition? Take the sentence: *A hammer is a tool. Hammer* is the term to be defined, and *tool* is a specific class word. But you still do not know exactly what a hammer is or does. To complete the definition, you need a **limiting feature.** A limiting feature is a word or phrase that distinguishes the term from other members of its class. A hammer is a tool that is used to drive in a nail. *Hammer* is still the term to be defined. *Tool* is still a specific class word, and the phrase *that is used to drive in a nail* is a limiting feature.

You sometimes need several limiting features to define a word. Read the following sentence that defines the term *jaguar: A jaguar is a large, spotted cat found in Central and South America.* The word *cat* is a specific class word. There are three limiting features: (1) the cat is large, (2) the cat is spotted, and (3) the cat is found in Central and South America. There are other large spotted cats in different parts of the world, and there are other large cats in Central and South America. Thus, you need all three limiting features to completely define the term *jaguar.*

Exercise 4   **Limiting Features**

Rewrite the sentences on the next page to form complete definitions. If you need help, choose limiting features from the list below.

around the earth	striped
birdlike	infectious
carried by mosquitoes	that runs east and west
domestic	large
that carries oxygen through the body	that purifies the blood
imaginary	with very little water
sandy	that may guard the house
surrounded on three sides by land	with scaly feathers

Section 3-1 Parts of a Definition, continued

a. Pterodactyls were reptiles.

Pterodactyls were birdlike reptiles with scaly feathers.

_____

b. A tiger is a cat.

A tiger is a large, striped cat.

_____

c. A dog is an animal.

A dog is a domestic animal that may guard the house.

_____

d. A desert is a region.

A desert is a sandy region with very little water.

_____

e. A bay is a body of water.

A bay is a body of water surrounded on three sides by land.

_____

f. Latitude is a line.

Latitude is an imaginary line around Earth that runs east and west.

_____

g. Malaria is a disease.

Malaria is an infectious disease carried by mosquitoes.

_____

h. The liver is an organ.

The liver is an organ that purifies the blood.

_____

i. The circulatory system is a system.

The circulatory system is a system that carries oxygen through the

body._____

Section 3-1 Parts of a Definition, continued

Exercise 5   Dissecting a Definition

If the students need additional practice taking definitions apart to distinguish the three parts, have them choose a few terms that are defined within their textbooks. Have the students break these sentences apart as they did in Exercise 5.

It might also help to write a formal definition on the board, then use three different colors to mark the three different parts of the definition.

For each of the following sentences, list the term being defined, the class word (stating whether it is general, specific, or repetitive), and all of the limiting features. Note that there may be more lines than you need. Refer to Table 3-1 if needed.

a. A membrane-covered structure that contains all of the materials necessary for life is called a cell.

Term __cell__

Class word __structure (general)__

Limiting features

__membrane-covered__

__that contains all of the materials necessary for life__

_____

b. Lymph nodes are small, bean-shaped organs that work like nets to remove particles from the lymph.

Term __lymph nodes__

Class word __organs (specific)__

Limiting features

__small__

__bean-shaped__

__that work like nets to remove particles from the lymph__

c. A hanging valley is a small glacial valley that joins the deeper main valley.

Term __hanging valley__

Class word __valley (repetitive)__

Limiting features

__small__

__glacial__

__that joins the deeper main valley__

CHAPTER

3 | **DEFINITIONS**

3-2 Ways of Defining

Make sure that students understand that the parts of a definition from Section 3-1 apply only to formal definitions. Informal definitions frequently contain limiting features without explicitly stating a class word.

There are two main ways to define a term. The first is the way that you might find a term defined in a dictionary or glossary. When you look up a definition in the dictionary, you expect to see that definition stated very plainly. This definition is a **formal definition.** Formal definitions can also be found within a written text. Sentences that state exactly what a term means include a formal definition. The following three sentences are examples of formal definitions.

1. Ecology is the study of the complex relationships between living things and their environment. *(from Modern Earth Science)*
2. The transmission of characteristics from parents to their offspring is called heredity. *(from Holt Biology Visualizing Life)*
3. The word *compound* means a pure substance composed of two or more elements that are chemically combined.

Each of the formal definitions above contains the three parts of a definition described in Section 3-1: a term, a class word, and at least one limiting feature. The first sentence directly states what ecology *is*. This type of definition is probably the most common form of a formal definition. The second example tells you what the transmission of characteristics *is called*. In this way, it gives a formal definition of the term *heredity*. The third example tells you what something *means*. Most formal definitions will fit one of these patterns.

When we speak, we usually use **informal definitions.** An informal definition uses the minimum number of words to convey an accurate definition. You will frequently see informal definitions in your textbooks. These definitions are commonly written as parenthetical, or explanatory, phrases following the important term. The sentence below is an example of this type of informal definition.

An energy transfer often leads to an energy conversion, a change from one form of energy into another. *(from Holt Science and Technology: Physical Science)*

Any definition is considered informal if it does not contain all three of the parts described in Section 3-1. Consider the sentence: *Coasting is being able to move without using any energy.* Which part is missing? *Coasting* is the term to be defined. The phrase *being able to move without using any energy* is a limiting feature. There is no class word in the sentence. However, you still understand the full meaning of the term *coasting*.

You should note that the word *when* is frequently misused in informal definitions. As you learned in Chapter 2, *when* is a time marker. Read the following sentence: *Coasting is when you're able to move without using any energy.* The term *coasting* is being defined. There is no time frame in the definition. Therefore, if a definition does not involve time, the word *when* should be avoided.

Section 3-2 Ways of Defining, continued

This passage is available on **Transparency 12.** Begin a discussion of the many ways an author can define a term by asking students to figure out how many different ways the author of this passage defines terms.

In comparing the formal and informal definitions in this exercise, ask students for the term, class word, and limiting features of each formal definition. You may wish to use different-colored markers to underline each part of the formal definition. This way, students can easily see the difference between the formal and informal definitions in the passage.

Exercise 6 **Formal or Informal?**

The following passage contains eight terms that are defined within the passage. In the spaces provided, determine whether each definition is formal or informal.

Ecology

Earth scientists primarily study the **geosphere,** the solid Earth; the **hydrosphere,** its water; and the **atmosphere,** the gases surrounding Earth. Other scientists, called **biologists,** study the living world. An area of science in which biology and Earth science are closely linked is called ecology. **Ecology** is the study of the complex relationships between living things and their environment.

Organisms on Earth inhabit many different environments. A community of organisms and the environment they inhabit is called an **ecosystem.** The terms *ecology* and *ecosystem* come from the Greek word *oikos,* meaning "house."

The largest ecosystem is called the **biosphere.** The biosphere encompasses all life on Earth and the physical environment that supports it. The biosphere extends from the ocean depths to the atmosphere a few kilometers above Earth's surface.

A tropical rain forest is one example of a large ecosystem within the biosphere. Plants in the rain forest use sunlight to produce food through a process known as **photosynthesis.**

(from Modern Earth Science)

a. geosphere   informal

b. hydrosphere   informal

c. atmosphere   informal

d. biologists   formal

e. ecology   formal

f. ecosystem   formal

g. biosphere   formal

h. photosynthesis   formal

Name_____ Date _____ Class_____

Exercise 7 Writing Formal Definitions

Ask students which was more difficult—writing formal definitions or writing informal definitions. It is likely that students will have less difficulty writing formal definitions because they have a definite model, or set of instructions, to follow. Point out to them, however, that they have no trouble coming up with informal definitions in their everyday speech. They just do not normally think about how they are defining words when they speak.

Study the drawing of an adult human and write a paragraph containing formal definitions for the following terms:

skull

clavicle

ribs

patella

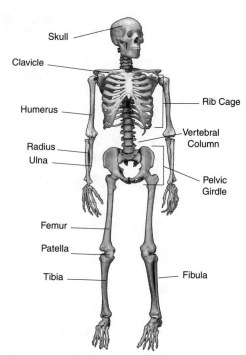

Students' answers will vary. The following is a sample of a correct answer. The skull is a bone that gives structure to the human head. It surrounds the brain. The clavicle is the part of the skeleton also called the collar bone. The ribs are the bones that surround the chest cavity. The patella is a floating bone also known as the knee cap.

_____

_____

Exercise 8 Writing Informal Definitions

Write a paragraph that contains informal definitions for the following terms: duck, egg, duckling, webbed feet

Students' answers will vary. The following is a sample of a correct answer. Ducks are frequently found in lakes. They have webbed feet that help them swim. Ducks are also able to fly which allows them to be migratory birds. Ducks give birth to their young by laying eggs. When the eggs hatch, ducklings, or baby ducks, emerge.

_____

CHAPTER

3   DEFINITIONS

3-3 Deeper Understanding

You have probably memorized many definitions in your school career. Vocabulary tests are common in most subjects. But did you *really* understand the full meaning of those words whose definitions you memorized? Understanding a word does not mean simply being able to define it. It also means knowing how the word relates to larger topics. Often, knowing how the word relates to larger topics involves putting the word in context.

Many basic definitions are given in one sentence, as you have seen throughout the first two parts of this chapter. Sometimes, an author may use several sentences or several paragraphs to fully define a term or a concept. In this case, the definition becomes an **expanded definition.**

The passage on glaciers can be found on **Transparency 13.** Using a colored pen, mark the first sentence as the formal definition. Point out to students that the passage **classifies** glaciers into two types. Classification is frequently an important part of an expanded definition. You may wish to use a different-colored pen to underline sentences and phrases involved in classification.

Point out that the author also cites examples of glacier locations. Examples can be another tool to create an expanded definition. A pen of a third color could highlight these sentences on the transparency. Classification and examples are important topics and will be discussed more thoroughly in Chapters 4 and 9, respectively.

Take a look at the following expanded definition of the word *glacier.* Notice that the author gives a simple formal definition in the first sentence. Then the author continues by distinguishing between the two different types of glaciers. The passage places glaciers in the context of their geographic positions. After you have finished reading the passage, you should have a fairly clear mental picture of both types of glaciers.

Glaciers

Glaciers are masses of moving ice. There are two main types of glaciers; they are distinguished by their size and where they are formed. One type of glacier is formed in mountainous areas. As the ice moves down a valley, it produces a *valley glacier,* which is a long, narrow, wedge-shaped mass of ice. Valley glaciers are best developed in the high mountainous regions of the world, such as in coastal Alaska, the Himalayas, the Andes, the Alps, and New Zealand.

The other type of glacier covers large land areas. These masses of ice, called *continental ice sheets,* occupy millions of square kilometers. Today, continental ice sheets are found only in Greenland and Antarctica.

(from Modern Earth Science)

Think back to Chapter 1 of this text. The author uses many of the descriptive strategies mentioned in Chapter 1 to describe glaciers. Definitions are basically descriptions of terms. Spatial patterns and figurative language will help you write expanded definitions.

Read the following passage. While you read, think about all of the descriptive strategies used by the author to define the term *fog.*

Section 3-3 Deeper Understanding, continued

The passage is available on **Transparency 14.** You may wish to use colored pens to point out the sentences containing comparison, contrast, and classifications. The first sentence is a comparison sentence. The second describes a similarity and asks the students to infer the difference.

Fog

Fog, like clouds, is the result of the condensation of water vapor in the air. The chief difference between fog and clouds is that fog forms very near the surface of Earth when air close to the ground is cooled. For example, you may be familiar with one type of fog that results from the nightly cooling of Earth. This type of fog is called *ground fog.* Ground fog usually forms on calm, clear nights. It is thickest in valleys and low-lying places because the dense, cold air in which it forms sinks to the lower elevations.

Two other types of fog often form inland. An *upslope fog* is formed by the lifting and cooling of air as it rises along land slopes. Upslope fog is really a kind of cloud formation at ground level. A type of fog known as *steam fog* usually forms over inland rivers and lakes. Steam fog is a shallow layer of fog formed when cool air moves over a warm body of water.

(from Modern Earth Science)

The author's main strategy in defining *fog* is to compare fog to something similar, in this case clouds. Notice that each type of fog is placed in the context of where it forms. This second strategy uses spatial relationships described in Chapter 1. The third type of description used in this expanded definition discusses how the three varieties of fog form. In other words, it classifies fog into three different types. Exercise 9 gives you more practice finding description strategies in an expanded definition. Then, Exercise 10 will give you the opportunity to write some expanded definitions.

Exercise 9   Expanded Definitions

Read the following passage, and discuss the strategies that the author uses to expand the definition of the term *meteoroid.*

Shooting Stars

The passage "Shooting Stars" is available on **Transparency 15.** You might wish to underline sections of the passage while you discuss the different description techniques used in the expanded definition. Point out the formal definition, any comparisons or contrasts, and a spatial relationship.

A meteoroid is a small, rocky body orbiting the sun. Meteoroids are similar to asteroids, but they are much smaller. In fact, most meteoroids probably come from asteroids. When a meteoroid falls into Earth's atmosphere, it is usually traveling at such a high speed that its surface heats up and melts. As it burns up, the meteoroid glows and gives off an enormous amount of light and heat. From the ground, we see a spectacular streak of light, or a shooting star.

(from Holt Science and Technology: Physical Science)

Section 3-3 Deeper Understanding, continued

First, the author gives a formal definition for the term meteoroid. Then,

he or she compares meteoroids to asteroids. This comparison includes a

reference to the size of meteoroids. Finally, the author describes what

meteoroids do as they enter Earth's atmosphere. This description uses a

spatial relationship (the relationship between the meteoroid and the sun

and between the meteoroid and Earth), and a description of what a

falling meteoroid, or shooting star, looks like.

_____

_____

_____

_____

_____

_____

_____

_____

_____

Exercise 10 Writing Expanded Definitions

Write an expanded definition of each of the following words. If you
like, make one or two comparisons.

a. soccer

Students answers will vary. The following is an example of a correct

response. Soccer is a sport in which two teams try to kick a round ball

into the other team's net, or goal. Most of the world calls soccer "foot-

ball," but in the United States we have a different sport that we call

football. Soccer is like a combination of hockey and football. As in

hockey, the two teams have a net guarded by a goalie at the end of the

Students having trouble with Exercise 10 could be encouraged to write an expanded definition of their favorite sport or hobby. The familiar subject matter might help them focus on the exercise and not on the terms themselves.

Section 3-3 Deeper Understanding, continued

playing area. Like football, soccer is played on a grassy field, usually out-

doors.

_____

_____

_____

_____

_____

_____

b. moon

Answers will vary. A sample correct answer follows. A moon is a natural

satellite orbiting a planet. Earth has one moon. Most other planets also

have moons. Earth's moon is like a giant round rock without an atmos-

phere. Jupiter has a moon that is similar to a huge ball of ice.

_____

_____

_____

_____

_____

_____

_____

_____

_____

Section 3-3 Deeper Understanding, continued

c. DNA

Answers will vary. A sample correct answer follows. DNA is deoxyribose

nucleic acid. It is a biochemical that is responsible for transmitting all

genetic information. DNA looks like a ladder that has been twisted. The

sides of the ladder are made up of sugar and phosphate molecules. The

rungs of the ladder are made of the nucleic-acid bases. Each rung con-

tains two bases that join together to connect the ladder.

_____

_____

_____

_____

_____

GLOSSARY

class word the class or category to which a term belongs (39)

etymology the study of the origin of a word (37)

expanded definition a longer definition that takes several sentences or paragraphs (47)

formal definition a definition that contains a term, a class word,
and one or more limiting features (37)

general class word a class word that is difficult to visualize, such
as device, science, or method (39)

informal definition a short definition that contains a minimum
amount of information (44)

limiting feature a word or phrase that distinguishes the term from
other members of its class (41)

repetitive class word a class word that is the same as the term, or
part of the term, being defined (39)

specific class word a class word that is easy to visualize, such as
tool, animal, or metal (39)

term the word that is being defined (37)

4-1 Why Do We Classify?

Classification is one of the most important ways we have to organize our world. It is the way we make sense of the hundreds and thousands of things around us. Stop and think for a moment. What are some everyday ways we classify things? Some people you know are friends; others are not friends. Some of your subjects are hard; others are easy. Some things you do are work; others are play. Without being aware of it, you put most things in your life into categories.

Classification takes a very complicated world and tries to simplify it by putting things into categories. Think about how difficult it would be to eat a healthy diet if foods were not put into nutritional categories. If the categories shown in **Figure 4-1:** fats, dairy, vegetables, fruits, meats, and grains did not exist, how would you know what foods to eat in which amounts? Things could get very confusing. For this reason classifying is important.

Classifying is also one of the most important tools of scientific thinking. The world of science encompasses everything, from the smallest particle inside an atom to a distant galaxy. If scientists did not divide the universe into smaller categories, they would never be able to understand much of it. One way they have divided the universe into smaller categories is by separating things into different subject areas, such as biology (life science), Earth science, and physical science.

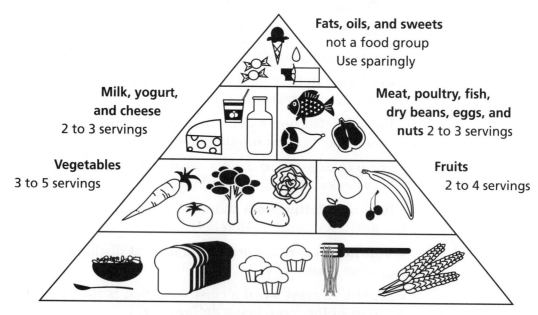

FIGURE 4-1 The food pyramid classifies different types of food.

Section 4-1 Why Do We Classify?, continued

In Chapter 3, you studied how an accurate definition leads to the understanding of a term or idea. Classifying is closely related to defining. Often a term is defined by the category to which it belongs. Take the following example that helps you understand the vast field of physics by defining its two main branches: *classical* and *modern* physics. Classical physics includes everything that physicists knew before 1900. Modern physics deals with the things that physicists have discovered since 1900.

There are often many different ways to classify the same thing. Two people can look at the same objects and classify them very differently. If you do not think so, think of all the different ways to classify the letters of the alphabet.

A B C D E F G H I J K L M
N O P Q R S T U V W X Y Z

One way to classify the letters of the alphabet is to group them by letters that have curves in them—B, C, D, G, J, O, P, Q, R, S, and U; and letters without curves—A, E, H, I, K, L, M, N, T, V, W, X, Y, Z. Exercise 1 challenges you to think about the many different ways you can classify the letters of the alphabet.

Exercise 1   Classification

How many other ways can you think of to classify the capital letters of the alphabet? Write your categories in the spaces below.

a. vowels and consonants

_____

b. open letters (e.g., C, G, H) and closed letters (e.g., B, D, Q)

_____

c. letters that can also be a word (A and I) and letters that cannot

_____

d. letters used for report-card grades and letters not used for report

card grades

e. mirror images (e.g., A, H, I, M) and nonmirror images

_____

Name _____ Date _____ Class _____

4-2 The Direction of Classifying

Begin a class discussion comparing bottom-up and top-down processes by asking students to use a bottom-up process to classify the terms *pen, pencil, book,* and *notebook.* Then have students use a top-down process to classify items found on a kitchen table.

Classifying involves finding things that have something in common and *grouping* them into a **class** or **category.** That *something in common* is the **basis for classification.** For example, you could group *coal, oil,* and *gas* as energy sources. Coal, oil, and gas are members of the class *energy sources.* This method of classifying takes specific items (coal, oil, and gas) and finds a more general word, or a class word, that describes all of them. This method of classifying is called a **bottom-up process** (↑). It goes from the specific to the general.

ENERGY SOURCES

coal   oil   gas   wind   water

You can also classify items in the other direction. Instead of starting with specific items and thinking of a general category, you can start with a general category and then think of specific items in that category. Take, for example, the word *alloy.* An alloy is a mixture that contains two or more metals. If *alloy* is the general class word, then specific items in the class might include bronze, brass, and steel. This method of classifying is called a **top-down process** (↓). It goes from the general to the specific.

ALLOY

bronze   brass   steel

At different levels, the same term can be specific (a member of a class) *and* general (a class word). In the previous example, *alloy* was used as a class word. *Alloy* can also be a member of the class *metals.* At the same time, *alloy* is both specific and general, depending on the basis for classification, a concept you will examine shortly.

Take the concept of *elements* in chemistry as another example. The word *element* can be a class word. There are 112 known elements, including carbon, oxygen, and nitrogen. But the word *elements* can also be a member of a higher class, *pure substances.* In turn, *pure substances* can serve as both a class word and a specific member. **Figure 4-2** shows how a **classification tree** can be used to analyze many levels of classes and their members. The classification tree makes up a **taxonomy,** or a top-down diagram that gets more specific at each lower level.

Section 4-2 The Direction of Classifying, continued

FIGURE 4-2 DIFFERENT CLASSES OF MATTER

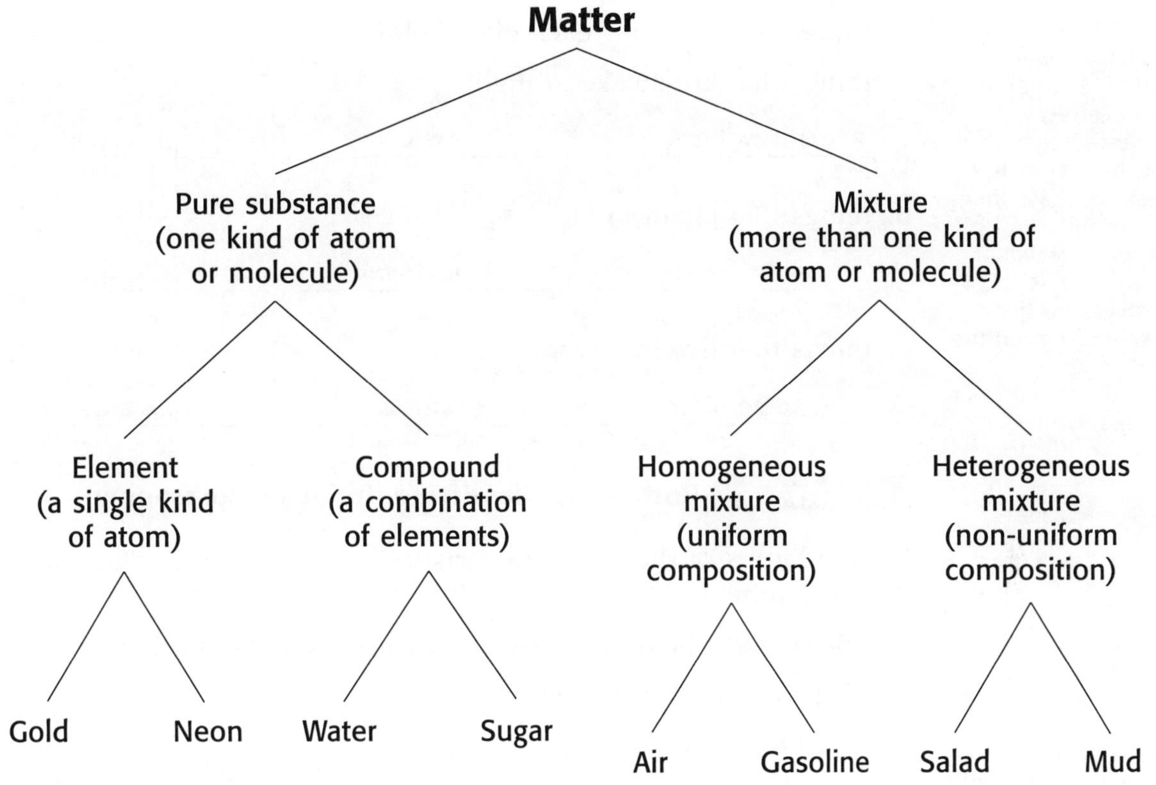

Matter

Pure substance
(one kind of atom
or molecule)

Mixture
(more than one kind of
atom or molecule)

Element
(a single kind
of atom)

Compound
(a combination
of elements)

Homogeneous
mixture
(uniform
composition)

Heterogeneous
mixture
(non-uniform
composition)

Gold   Neon   Water   Sugar   Air   Gasoline   Salad   Mud

The classification tree shown in Figure 4-2 is available on **Transparency 16.** Ask students to try to go further down the taxonomy. For example, have them classify types of gasoline or sugar. You can also have them develop this taxonomy from the bottom up.

Reasoning from the general to the specific is called **deductive reasoning.** Figure 4-2 shows an example of deductive reasoning. A top-down classification is based on deductive reasoning. Reasoning from the specific to the general is called **inductive reasoning.** A bottom-up classification is based on inductive reasoning. Stop for a moment and compare the different terms by studying **Table 4-1.** Exercises 2 and 3 will give you practice using the two directions of classifying.

TABLE 4-1 THE DIRECTION OF CLASSIFYING

Direction of classifying	Description of process	Type of reasoning	How to classify
Top-down ↓	general-to-specific	deductive	start with a class word, then determine specific members
Bottom-up ↑	specific-to-general	inductive	start with a specific member, then determine a general class word

Section 4-2 The Direction of Classifying, continued

Exercise 2   Top-Down Classifying: Deductive Reasoning

Students' answers will vary. The answers given here are examples of correct answers. After students have completed the exercise, ask them to think about whether they would have been able to go the other direction (bottom-up) given the members they selected, but not given the class words.

List three members for each class below.

a. things that are awake at night

   night watchmen   owls   possums

b. things that change color

   some leaves   chameleons   the sky

c. things that live in trees

   some birds   squirrels   some mosses

Exercise 3   Bottom-Up Classifying (Inductive Reasoning)

If Exercise 3 is too hard, read one set of five related items and have the students guess the class. Students should note that we are much more accustomed to deductive reasoning and that deductive reasoning seems much easier than inductive reasoning.

Put the letters of the 10 characteristics below into two categories, and determine what two objects the characteristics describe.

   a. Some have pictures in them, and others just contain words.

   b. It has various numbers on its face.

   c. Early kinds of it took years to produce.

   d. It may use electrical, battery, or mechanical power.

   e. Some are worn as jewelry.

   f. Its main parts are usually held together by glue.

   g. Early kinds of this object used sand or sun.

   h. It has hands.

   i. It has a spine and a cover.

   j. It is made of paper.

Members of Category 1   a   i

                              c   j

                              f

Object 1 a book

Members of Category 2   b   g

                              d   h

                              e

Object 2 a watch or clock

Exercise 4 Completing Taxonomies

Fill in the empty spaces in these taxonomies (classification trees).

The blank trees are available on **Transparencies 17 and 18.** Use the exercise as a class activity by filling in the blanks as students offer answers. Keep in mind that there are many possible answers for some of the blanks.

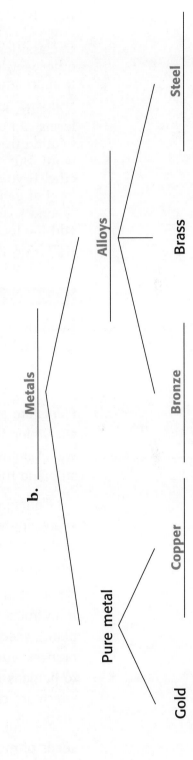

a.

Tools

Screwdriver   Hammer   Saw   Drill

Saw: Circular saw   Jig saw

b.

Metals

Pure metal   Alloys

Pure metal: Gold   Copper

Alloys: Bronze   Brass   Steel

CHAPTER

4 **CLASSIFYING AND CATEGORIZING**

4-3 Levels of Generality

Look back at what you have learned about bottom-up and top-down classifying. The taxonomy shown in Figure 4-2 has four levels of classification. These levels are called **levels of generality.** In other words, they go from the general (at the top of the taxonomy) to more and more specific (at the bottom of the taxonomy).

Figure 4-2 illustrates the concept of levels of generality. But these levels can exist in any classification whether or not a formal classification tree is drawn. The word *tool*, for example, is a general word. But the words *hammer, saw,* and *drill* are much more specific. If you were classifying tools, the word *tool* would be the first level of generality. The words *hammer, saw,* and *drill* would be the second level. If you wanted to classify tools even further, you could add the terms *coping saw, circular saw,* and *saber saw* under the term *saw*. These specific types of saws would make up the third level of generality.

Exercise 5   Identifying Levels of Generality

Transparency 19 contains a classification tree based on the levels of generality in this passage. After students have had a chance to attempt the exercise, analyze the passage along with the students using the overhead transparency.

Read the following passage, and list the levels of generality that are described in the text, using the spaces that follow on the next page.

Some Scoop on Plants

Plants are an essential part of our lives. The word *plants* includes everything from grass and flowers to trees and bushes. This passage will examine some of the uses of plants. After reading the passage, stop and think about where we would be without plants.

Plants produce oxygen. They also provide us with food; almost everything we eat comes from a plant or an animal that ate a plant. And plants provide us with many other useful products, such as wood, medicines, fibers for making cloth and paper, and rubber.

Did you know that most of the food people eat actually comes from fruits? Fruits are the parts of a flowering plant that contain the plant's seeds. When you think of fruits, you probably think of apples, oranges, and peaches. However, the fruits that provide the most food to humans come from the cereal grasses. The fruits of cereal grasses, which are called grains, include wheat, rice, corn, and oats.

The fruits of the pea or bean family have more protein than the seeds of most plants. These high-protein seeds include lentils and soybeans. Soybeans can be cooked and pressed into cakes called tofu or bean curd.

(from Holt Biology Visualizing Life)

Section 4-3 Levels of Generality, continued

1. uses of plants

2. oxygen, food, wood, medicine, fibers, or rubber

3. fruits

4. cereal grains or beans

5. wheat, rice, corn, or oats; lentils or soybeans

6. tofu, or bean curd

Analyzing the Levels of Generality

You have already seen that a classification can have several levels of generality. The taxonomy on classes of matter shown in Figure 4-2 had four levels of generality. The classification of useful plants in Exercise 5 had six levels. To really understand the process of classifying, you should NOT mix the levels of generality or include items in a class to which they do not belong. Consider the following simple example:

radio   television   newspaper   magazine   airplane

The first four items belong to the category *media*. The word *airplane* does not.

Often, you will be asked to create a classification from the bottom up using inductive reasoning. To do so, think of how the items to be classified are related. For example, how are the following words related?

bicycle   car   bus   truck   motorcycle

They all belong to the class *kinds of transportation.* So, there are two levels of generality.

Level 1: kinds of transportation

Level 2: bicycle, car, bus, truck, motorcycle

But you can classify the items further by adding more levels of generality. For instance, you could divide them into the categories *motorized* and *nonmotorized*.

Level 1:   kinds of transportation

Level 2:   motorized   nonmotorized

Level 3: car, bus, truck, motorcycle   bicycle

Section 4-3 Levels of Generality, continued

Or you could divide them into two-wheeled and four-wheeled kinds of transportation.

Level 1:   kinds of transportation

Level 2: two-wheeled   four-wheeled

Level 3: bicycle, motorcycle   bus, truck, car

Using either system provides three levels of classification. The way an author classifies—including the number of levels of classification—depends on the writer's purpose, the audience, and, of course, the subject matter.

Exercise 6   **Determining Levels of Generality**

Transparency 20 contains a classification tree based on the four levels of generality in this exercise. After students have had a chance to attempt the exercise, analyze the classification along with the students' responses using the overhead transparency.

Arrange the following list of words by levels of generality. There may be more answer blanks for levels than you need.

animals	crocodiles	mammals	tigers
apes	humans	monkeys	turtles
big cats	leopards	primates	owl
birds	lions	reptiles	

Level 1: _____ animals _____

Level 2: _____ birds, mammals, reptiles _____

Level 3: _____ owl; big cats, primates; turtles, crocodiles _____

_____

Level 4: _ leopards, lions, tigers; apes, humans, monkeys _____

_____

Level 5: _____

_____

Exercise 7   **Analyzing the Levels of Generality**

Draw a classification tree for the items below using the space provided on the next page. How many levels of generality does your tree have?

food	meat
name-brand orange juice	dairy products
vegetables	generic orange juice
grapefruit juice	juices
orange juice	

Number of Levels: _____ 4 _____

Name_____ Date _____ Class _____

Section 4-3 Levels of Generality, continued

Transparency 21 contains a classification tree based on the levels of generality in this exercise. After students have had a chance to attempt the exercise, review the answer with the students using the overhead transparency.

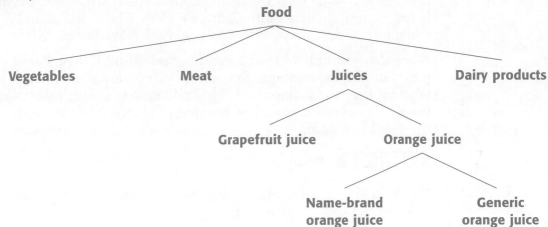

Section 4-3 Levels of Generality, continued

Overlap

Sometimes an item in a classification can belong to more than one class. In this case, there is *overlap*. Do you remember Exercise 1 that asked you to classify the letters of the alphabet? One classification system might divide the letters into *open* and *closed* letters. The letter C would obviously be an open letter. The letter D would obviously be a closed letter. However, the letters A and R seem to fall into both categories. Do they belong to the open-letter class, the closed-letter class, or a class of their own? Most often, when an overlap occurs, it is best to put the items into their own class. The letters A and R could form a new class, *letters that are both open and closed.*

Another example of overlap can be found in biology. Fungi (the plural of *fungus*) contain features of both plants *and* animals, so how are they to be classified? This dilemma is solved by classifying fungi as a separate group, or *kingdom*. Mushrooms are members of the fungi kingdom.

Exercise 8   Overlap

As an extension exercise, have the students create new categories for the overlapping items. Students could also practice creating taxonomies by drawing a classification tree with their final set of categories.

The following is a list of the equipment you might need to play baseball, football, and soccer.

cleats	shoulder pads	goal post
helmet	diamond	net
ball	mitt	shin guards
bat	base	

a. Group the objects into the following categories. Skip any items that belong to more than one category.

Football equipment	Soccer equipment	Baseball equipment
shoulder pads	net	bat
goal post	shin guards	mitt
		diamond
		base

b. List the items that overlap the categories in part (a), and tell which categories they overlap. If all three categories apply to an item, write *all three* in the first category column.

List of items	Category	Category
cleats	all three	
helmet	football	baseball
ball	all three	

CHAPTER

4 CLASSIFYING AND CATEGORIZING

4-4 Analyzing Text for Classification Patterns

There are six main parts to any classification. You were introduced to the first and sixth parts in Section 4-2 of this chapter: the *name of the class or category* and the *basis for classification*. Once an author gives the names of the categories, he or she usually uses a verb such as *divide* or *classify* to separate items into the given classes or categories. This is the second part of a classification.

Often, an author will list the *number of members* in a category. This step is the third part of a classification. The fourth part of a classification includes *classifying words*. These words help categorize the items being classified. **Classifying words** include *kinds, types, groups,* and *varieties*. The fifth part of a classification simply lists the specific members of the class.

Read the following passage, which describes the classification of rocks. The superscripted letters point out the many different parts of the classification. A list of these parts can be found below the passage. The words in parentheses on the list indicate the example of that part found in the reading passage.

On the Rocks

The passage is available on **Transparency 22.** Refer to the lettered words, phrases, and sentences on the transparency as you explain the various parts. Use colored pens to highlight the six parts of the classification.

Geologists study the forces and processes that act upon the rocks[a] of Earth's crust. Based on these studies, geologists have classified[b] rocks into three[c] major types[d]: igneous[e], sedimentary[e], and metamorphic[e]. The classification is based on the way the rocks are formed[f]. Igneous rock forms when magma cools and hardens. Magma is called *lava* if it cools at Earth's surface. Sedimentary rock is formed when fragments of rock, minerals, and organic matter harden after being compressed and cemented together. The word *metamorphic* means "changed form." Metamorphic rocks come from other rocks that are changed by certain forces and processes, including tremendous pressure, extreme heat, and chemical processes. Any of the three major types of rock can be changed into another type.

(from Modern Earth Science)

a. the topic or *name* of the class (rocks)
b. a *verb* such as classify, divide, separate, categorize, group, arrange (have classified)
c. the *number of members* in the class (three)
d. a plural *classifying word:* kinds, types, categories, classes, divisions, groups, species, sorts, varieties (types)
e. *members of the class* (igneous, sedimentary, metamorphic)
f. the *basis for classification.* The basis tells how the members are different or alike and describes the features or qualities that distinguish one member of a class from another. (The classification is based on the way the rocks are formed.)

Section 4-4 Analyzing Text for Classification Patterns, continued

---

Some text descriptions contain all six parts of a classification. Others may be incomplete. The previous passage contains all of the possible parts of a classification. The different parts of a classification do not always appear in the same sequence, or order, in the reading passage. Sometimes you will need to look very closely at a passage to find the parts of a classification.

Exercise 9 **Text Analysis**

The passage is available on **Transparency 23**. Refer to the sentences on the transparency as you review the answers to the exercise. Use different-colored pens to highlight the different parts of the classification in the passage.

Read the following passage. Using the list of parts in a classification, give an example from the passage for each part on the lines provided. You are asked for two bases of classification.

What's Inside an Atom

As tiny as an atom is, it consists of three even smaller types of particles—protons, neutrons, and electrons. The particles can be distinguished by their location inside the atom. Protons and neutrons make up the nucleus, which is in the center of the atom. Electrons are found outside the nucleus.

The particles inside an atom can also be separated by charge. Protons are the positively charged particles of the nucleus. Neutrons are the particles of the nucleus that have no charge. Neutrons are slightly more massive than protons, but the difference in mass is very small. Electrons are the negatively charged particles in atoms. The current atomic theory states that electrons are found moving around the nucleus within electron clouds. The charges of protons and electrons are opposite but equal in size.

(from Holt Science and Technology: Physical Science)

a. name of class <u>parts of an atom</u>

b. verb <u>can be distinguished or can be separated</u>

c. number of members <u>three</u>

d. classifying word <u>types of particles</u>

e. members of the class <u>protons, neutrons, and electrons</u>

f. basis <u>location inside atom</u>

g. basis <u>charge</u>

Section 4-4 Analyzing Text for Classification Patterns, continued

Exercise 10   **Finding Bases**

The potentially danger-ous use of nuclear power causes nuclear power to overlap the dangerous and safe categories. Ask stu-dents if there should be another option besides dangerous or safe. Students may also think of other energy sources and classify them using the four bases for classifi-cation given in the passage.

Read the following passage, and determine the four bases for classification listed in the reading.

More Power to You

The world runs on energy. Cars, airplanes, factories, and your home all require energy. What are the different sources of energy, and what are some of the problems with them? For modern energy needs, we usually think of these five energy sources: fossil fuels, nuclear reactors, wind, the sun (solar energy), and water (hydroelectricity).

These various sources can be viewed, or classified, in different ways. Some are renewable. Others are nonrenewable. Nonrenewable sources cannot be replaced once they're used. Renewable sources can. Fossil fuels—coal, oil, and gas—are nonrenewable. Solar energy, wind, and hydroelectricity are all renewable. We can also think of energy sources as polluting and nonpolluting. Of all the energy sources, only fossil fuels are polluting.

Are energy resources dangerous? Fossil fuels are dangerous because they affect the air we breathe. Nuclear energy is potentially dangerous while the other energy sources are not. We can also view energy sources in terms of cost. Fossil fuels and nuclear energy are currently the least expensive. Solar, wind, and hydroelectricity are the most expensive.

(from Holt Environmental Science)

Fossil fuels

Hydroelectricity

Wind

Solar energy

a. <u>renewable or nonrenewable</u>

b. <u>polluting and nonpolluting</u>

c. <u>dangerous or safe</u>

d. <u>cost</u>

Section 4-4 Analyzing Text for Classification Patterns, continued

Exercise 11 Taxonomies from Text Analysis

Draw a classification tree based on the following passage.

The passage and a blank classification tree can be found on **Transparency 24.** After the students have had time to attempt the exercise, use different-colored pens to fill in the tree while high-lighting appropriate words and phrases in the passage. This will help students link the taxonomy to the written passage.

Ecosystems

Ecosystems are regions of the world that have similar plants, animals, and climates. Deserts, grasslands, forests, and tundras are some of the world's major ecosystems. There are also marine and savanna ecosystems.

Life, in its endless forms, dwells in the forests of the world. Like life itself, these forests have many faces. One type of forest we've been hearing a lot about lately is the tropical rain forest, with its towering trees and vines. Two other major forms are deciduous forests and taiga, also known as coniferous forests.

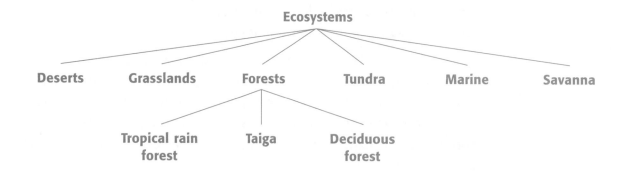

Section 4-4 Analyzing Text for Classification Patterns, continued

Exercise 12 **Reading for Classification**

You have already learned to use classification trees to get a picture of a classification. Tables can also be helpful in visualizing categories of items. Determine the bases for classifying forests, and fill in the table that follows. One block of the table is filled in for you as an example.

Forests

How do forest ecosystems differ? One way is in their location. Tropical rain forests are located in a belt around Earth near the equator. In contrast, deciduous forests generally occur between 30° and 50° north latitude, while coniferous forests, or taiga, stretch in a broad band across the Northern Hemisphere just below the Arctic Circle. As a result, tropical rain forests are always humid and wet, while deciduous regions can have extreme seasonal variations. In deciduous regions, summer temperatures can soar to 35°C (95°F), and winter temperatures often plummet well below freezing. Coniferous forests have short, cool summers and long, cold winters. Average subfreezing temperatures often plummet to –20°C (–4°F).

Coniferous forests also get very little precipitation (20–60 cm or 9–27 in.), most of which falls as snow. Deciduous forests are moist and receive 75–250 cm (34–114 in.) of precipitation annually. The tropical rain forests get about 250 cm (114 in.) of rain each year.

The rain and snow in a deciduous forest aid in the decomposition of fallen leaves and make the soil rich and deep. Conifer needles contain acidic substances, and when they die and fall, they acidify the soil. As a result, the soil of coniferous forests is less fertile. Rapid decay in tropical rain forests returns nutrients to the soil, but these nutrients are washed away by rainfall, so the soil is usually thin and poor. Still, the rain forest has the greatest variety of plants and animals of any region of the world. Deciduous forests have a wide variety of plants and animals, but not nearly as many as tropical rain forests have. Most plants cannot grow in acidic soil, which is one reason that coniferous forests have a limited variety of plants.

(from Holt Biology Visualizing Life, and Holt Environment Science)

Section 4-4 Analyzing Text for Classification Patterns, continued

	Bases For Classification				
Type of forest	Location	Annual precipitation	Climate	Soil	Variety of plant and animal life
Tropical rain forest	in a belt around the equator	250 cm	always warm and humid	thin and poor	greatest variety in the world
Temperate deciduous forest	30°–50° north latitude	75–250 cm	extreme seasonal variations—hot summers, cold winters	rich and deep	wide variety
Coniferous forest (taiga)	across the Northern Hemisphere just below the Arctic Circle	20–60 cm	short cool summers, long cold winters	acidic—not very fertile	limited variety

Section 4-4 Analyzing Text for Classification Patterns, continued

Sentence Patterns Used in Classifying

There are several patterns that writers use when they are classifying or categorizing information. These patterns fall into the same two groupings that you saw in Section 4-2: specific-to-general and general-to-specific. These patterns are summarized in **Table 4-2.** The passages you have already seen in this chapter contain sentences using some of these patterns. Notice that the pattern in item 5 is not complete. It leaves you wondering what types of rocks make up the three classes. Item 5 requires another sentence to give the reader a full understanding of the classification:

There are three categories of rocks. They include igneous, sedimentary, and metamorphic rocks.

TABLE 4-2 SENTENCE PATTERNS USED IN CLASSIFICATION

Specific-to-general				
1. Steel	is/are			an alloy. a metal.
2. Steel	is/are	a kind of a type of an example of a variety of		an alloy. a metal.
3. Steel	is can be may be	classified categorized classed	as	an alloy. a metal.
General-to-specific				
4. Rocks	is/are may be can be	divided separated arranged	into three	classes. groups. categories.
5. There are three		kinds types sorts classes categories	of	rocks.

Exercise 13 **Sentence Patterns**

Use each set of words to write two sentences. The first sentence should relate the words using a specific-to-general pattern. The second sentence should use a general-to-specific pattern.

a. soybeans, lentils, beans

specific-to-general: Soybeans and lentils are types of beans.

Section 4-4 Analyzing Text for Classification Patterns, continued

general-to-specific: Beans may be divided into categories such as soybeans and lentils.

b. inductive reasoning, deductive reasoning, reasoning

specific-to-general: Inductive reasoning and deductive reasoning are types of reasoning.

general-to-specific: Reasoning can be classified by two types: inductive reasoning and deductive reasoning.

c. gold, metal

specific-to-general: Gold is an example of a metal.

general-to-specific: Metals may be separated into types such as gold.

d. igneous, sedimentary, rock, metamorphic

specific-to-general: Igneous, sedimentary, and metamorphic are all classes of rocks.

general-to-specific: Rocks can be arranged into three classes: igneous, sedimentary, and metamorphic.

Exercise 14   **Developing Your Own Scheme**

This exercise could be assigned as homework to give students plenty of time for thinking creatively. Stress that this exercise should pull together everything they have learned throughout Chapter 4.

Try to invent an original classification and explain it in detail. Write out your answer using the lines on this and the following page. Use the example below as a model.

There are two kinds of people: *hoarders* and *chuckers*. Hoarders are people who never throw anything out. You can imagine what their rooms look like. Chuckers are people who are *always* throwing things out. What kinds of people are in your family? What kind of person are *you*?

Section 4-4 Analyzing Text for Classification Patterns, continued

_____

_____

_____

_____

_____

_____

_____

_____

GLOSSARY

basis for classification the system used to group members of a class, or the ways in which the members of a class are different or alike (54)

bottom-up process method of going from specific to general (54)

category a group of things that are alike in some way (54)

class a group of things that are alike in some way (54)

classification a grouping of things that are alike in some way (52)

classification tree a diagram that analyzes members of a class at more and more specific levels; a taxonomy (54)

classifying word a marker that indicates the presence of a classification (63)

deductive reasoning reasoning from the general to the specific, or top-down classifying (55)

inductive reasoning reasoning from the specific to the general, or bottom-up classifying (55)

levels of generality the different levels in a classification (58)

taxonomy a top-down diagram that is used for classifying, and that is more specific at each level (54)

top-down process method of going from general to specific (54)

CHAPTER

CAUSE-AND-EFFECT RELATIONSHIPS

5-1 Cause-and-Effect Markers

Introduce this chapter by providing from the students' science textbook examples in which words and patterns are used to illustrate cause-and-effect relationships. Consult Table 5-8 on page 88 for help in developing examples.

Cause-and-effect thinking is used to solve problems in everyday life: What caused the lights in your house to go out? What is going to happen as a result of your not studying for that exam? The first step in analyzing any problem is to find its cause.

A problem can have one cause or several causes. A cause may have one effect or several effects. Sometimes the cause of a problem is obvious or easy to find, sometimes it is very difficult. Sometimes the cause of a problem is impossible to find!

Cause-and-effect reasoning is also very important in science. It can be found in scientific descriptions. Cause-and-effect reasoning in science and in other subjects can often be identified by cause-and-effect words. Certain words are used to indicate cause or reason. Other words are used to indicate effect or result. **Table 5-1** gives common examples of both cause and effect words. These words are called **regular cause-and-effect markers.**

TABLE 5-1 REGULAR CAUSE-AND-EFFECT WORDS

Cause or reason		Effect or result	
cause	as a result of	accordingly	is an effect of
affect	because (of)	as a result	the result is
bring about	on account of	consequently	results from
produce	due to	for this reason	therefore
account for	is an influence on	hence	thus
generates		in order to	is produced by

Take a look at the following passage. Notice the boldfaced cause-and-effect markers. Think about how important cause-and-effect reasoning is in trying to answer the question of what happened to the dinosaurs.

Mass Extinctions

Some of the important divisions in the geologic time scale are marked by events that **caused** many animal and plant species to die out completely, or become extinct. There are several periods in Earth's history when a large number of species died out at the same time. These periods of large-scale extinction are called mass extinctions.

Scientists are not sure what **brings about** mass extinctions. Mass extinctions may **result from** major changes in Earth's climate. Some scientists think the mass extinction of the dinosaurs was **due to** a meteorite colliding with Earth and **causing** catastrophic climate changes.

(from Holt Science and Technology: Life Science)

Section 5-1 Cause-and-Effect Markers, **continued**

Exercise 1   Cause-and-Effect Words

The passage including the blank spaces can be found on **Transparency 27.** Use this transparency to review the correct answers with the students. Some of the markers are interchangeable (e.g., *causes* and *produces*). Point out this interchangeability as you fill in the blanks on the overhead.

Choose appropriate cause-and-effect words or phrases from the list, and write them in the blank spaces in the passage below. Use each word or phrase only once.

result (noun)	produces	because
is affected	bring about	because of
causes		

_____Because of_____ the Earth's curvature, the direct rays of the sun striking near the equator are more effective in heating an area than the slanting rays striking the polar regions. As a _____result_____, the polar regions receive much less heat.

_____Because_____ Earth receives more solar energy at the equator than at the poles, there is a belt of low air pressure at the equator. The heated air in the region of the equator is constantly rising. At the poles, the colder air is heavier and tends to sink. This sinking of cold air _____produces_____ regions of high atmospheric pressure.

Pressure differences in the atmosphere at the equator and at the poles _____bring about_____ a general movement of air worldwide. The circulation of the atmosphere _____is affected_____ by the rotation of Earth on its axis. The rotation _____causes_____ surface winds in the Northern Hemisphere to be deflected to the right and those in the Southern Hemisphere to be deflected to the left. This motion is called the Coriolis effect, after the nineteenth-century French mathematician who first described it.

(from Modern Earth Science)

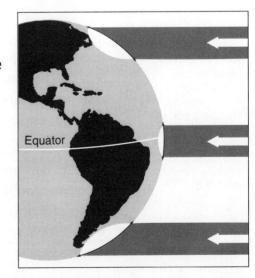

Equator

READING SKILLS WORKSHEETS   **73**

Special Cause-and-Effect Markers

Cause-and-effect relationships are often indicated by regular cause-and-effect markers. These markers include the words and phrases found in Table 5-1. It is fairly easy to identify regular cause-and-effect markers. Without regular markers these relationships are not so obvious.

A written cause-and-effect relationship may use **special cause-and-effect markers,** or words or phrases that indicate a cause-and-effect relationship but are not thought of as regular cause-and-effect words. As a result, it may be harder to recognize the cause-and-effect relationship in sentences containing special markers. **Table 5-2** lists some of these special markers and gives examples of sentences that use them to show cause-and-effect relationships.

TABLE 5-2 SPECIAL CAUSE-AND-EFFECT MARKERS

Word or Phrase	Example
creates	Air flowing toward the equator *creates* the trade winds.
is responsible for	The rotation of Earth on its axis *is responsible for* currents in the oceans and in the atmosphere.
has conferred	The energy revolution *has conferred* many benefits on modern society.

The following passage contains 2 regular cause-and-effect markers, and 5 special cause-and-effect markers. Can you find them? Note that not all of the special cause-and-effect markers can be found in Table 5-2.

Rubber

The first paragraph contains 3 cause-and-effect markers: *produce* (regular), *when* (special), and *making it* (special). The second paragraph contains 2 special markers: *creates* and *enabled*.

Rubber trees produce natural rubber. But natural rubber has relatively few practical applications. When warmed, individual molecules of natural rubber slide easily back and forth past each other. The rubber gets soft and gooey, making it useless for many purposes.

A process converting natural rubber into a useful commercial product was accidentally discovered by Charles Goodyear in 1839. Goodyear found that the addition of sulfur to molten rubber creates a material that remains very hard and tough when cooled. He called this process vulcanization. Vulcanization enabled rubber to be used in a wide variety of products, such as hoses, rainwear, and tires.

Section 5-1 Cause-and-Effect Markers, continued

The third paragraph contains 2 markers: *is responsible for* (special) and *caused* (regular).

In the first year of World War II, Japan controlled large portions of Southeast Asia. Southeast Asia is responsible for most of the world's natural rubber production. This caused the United States and other Allied nations to develop synthetic substitutes for natural rubber. Some synthetic rubbers have superior properties to natural rubber.

(from Modern Chemistry)

Exercise 2   Special Cause-and-Effect Markers

Read the following passage and list all cause-and-effect markers, both regular and special, in the spaces provided. Also, determine if the marker is regular or special. There may be more spaces than you need.

The passage can be found on **Transparency 28.** Use colored pens to highlight the different cause-and-effect markers. Point out that there are many different possibilities for special markers. Note that the distinction between regular and special markers can be slight.

What Holds You Up?

Water is about 1,000 times denser than air. Because of water's density, you can float on your back in a pool. For some aquatic animals, water provides much of the support necessary to keep their bodies from collapsing under the pull of gravity. For this reason, a jellyfish stranded on the beach cannot maintain its shape.

A variety of adaptations allows animals that left the sea to overcome the loss of physical support. In vertebrates, the skeleton is largely responsible for support of the body. A land animal's skeleton holds up its body against gravity much like beams and girders hold up a skyscraper.

Limbs play an important role in supporting vertebrates on land. When a terrestrial animal is standing, its legs bear the entire weight of its body. In this way, legs function like the pillars that hold up the roof of a building. Unlike pillars, however, animal legs have flexible joints that enable them to move.

(from Holt Biology Visualizing Life)

Because of, regular _____   is largely responsible for, special _____

provides, special _____   play an important role, special _____

For this reason, regular _____   enable, special _____

allow, special _____   _____

5-2 Cause-and-Effect Patterns

Multiple Causes and Effects

There are many factors influencing why a plant does or does not flower as it should. The plant may not be getting enough light, the temperature might be too high or too low, or the amount of moisture could be wrong. This is an example of a process that has multiple causes.

It is also possible for one cause to have multiple effects. The single explosion that is referred to as the big bang may have caused the creation of every planet, star, or other celestial body in the universe. That one event set in motion all other events that have followed it. The following two sentences give very clear examples of multiple causes and multiple effects. The numbers in each sentence point out each of the multiple causes or effects.

> **Multiple Causes.** (1) Patterns of vegetation and (2) action of wind account for the movement of earth and sand in desert regions.
>
> **Multiple Effects.** Convection (warm, rising air) is responsible for (1) high winds and (2) much of the rain in desert regions.

As an additional exercise, have students determine whether each example in the table shows multiple causes or multiple effects.

Table 5-3 lists some words and phrases that are used to indicate multiple causes or multiple effects.

TABLE 5-3 WORDS AND PHRASES USED IN MULTIPLE CAUSES AND EFFECTS

Word or Phrase	Example
also	Movements of air govern the pattern of rainfall. The arrangement of land masses is *also* an influence.
in addition (to)	Wind patterns are caused by heat from the sun. *In addition,* they are influenced by the rotation of Earth.
both/and	The Gulf Stream is responsible for the warmth of *both* the British Isles *and* western Norway.
an additional	The location of land masses is *an additional* influence on rainfall.
not only but also	The distribution of heat from the sun is responsible *not only* for wind *but also* for the major ocean currents.
moreover	*Moreover,* several other kinds of chemicals destroy ozone.

Section 5-2 Cause-and-Effect Patterns, continued

Read the passage below. It contains examples of multiple causes and effects.

Destruction of the Ozone Layer

The major culprit of (effect 1) ozone destruction is a class of chemicals called (cause 1) chlorofluorocarbons (CFCs). High over the South and North Poles, where it is very cold, CFCs stick to frozen water vapor and catalyze the conversion of ozone, O_3, into molecular oxygen, O_2. Moreover, (cause 2) several other kinds of chemicals destroy ozone. Because the amount of ozone in the upper atmosphere has fallen, (effect 2) more ultraviolet radiation is reaching Earth's surface. Also, scientists expect (effect 3) more cases of diseases caused by exposure to ultraviolet radiation: skin cancer, cataracts (a disorder in which the lens of the eye becomes cloudy), and cancer of the retina, (the light-sensitive part of the eye).

(from Biology Principles and Explorations)

Exercise 3 **Multiple Causes and Effects**

Write down the cause-and-effect formulas found in the following passage. Use the + symbol to indicate multiple causes. Use an arrow to show the cause-and-effect relationship. The first formula is written for you as an example.

Weathering and Erosion

The change in physical form or chemical composition of rock materials exposed at Earth's surface is called weathering. Mechanical weathering and chemical weathering are responsible for these changes.

When carbon dioxide from the air dissolves in water, a weak acid solution called carbonic acid is produced. When some minerals come in contact with carbonic acid, they combine chemically with the acid and form a new product. For example, carbonic acid reacts with calcite, which is a major component of limestone, and converts it to calcium bicarbonate. Calcium bicarbonate dissolves easily in water. The dissolving action of carbonic acid on limestone sometimes produces underground caverns.

One result of weathering is the formation of regolith, the layer of weathered rock fragments covering much of Earth's surface. Beneath the regolith lies the solid, unweathered rock that we call bedrock. Eventually the uppermost rock fragments weather and form a layer of

Section 5-2 Cause-and-Effect Patterns, continued

Discuss with the students the types of cause-and-effect relationships found in the passage after they have had ample opportunity to write down the formulas describing the relationships.

a. multiple causes, special marker

b. regular marker

c. multiple causes, special marker

d. special marker

e. regular marker

f. regular marker

g. special marker

h. special marker

i. multiple causes, regular marker

j. special marker

You may wish to point out that (i) and (j) make up a cause-and-effect series. This topic will be discussed later in the chapter.

very fine particles. This layer of small rock particles becomes soil. Soil is a complex mixture of minerals, water, gases, and the remains of dead organisms. As plants and animals die, their remains decay and produce humus, a dark organic material that enriches the soil.

(from Modern Earth Science)

a. *mechanical weathering + chemical weathering → changes in rock materials*

b. carbon dioxide from the air dissolves in water → carbonic acid is produced

c. some minerals come in contact with carbonic acid + combine chemically → new product

d. carbonic acid reacts with calcite → calcium bicarbonate

e. dissolving action of carbonic acid on limestone → underground caverns

f. weathering → regolith

g. uppermost rock fragment weather → layer of very fine particles

h. layers of small rock particles → soil

i. plants and animals die + their remains decay → humus

j. humus → enriched soil

Section 5-2 Cause-and-Effect Patterns, continued

Partial Causes and Degrees of Influence

Partial cause is related to the idea of multiple causes and-effects. Something may have an influence on an outcome, but it may not be the only cause, or even the most important cause, of that outcome. For example, if farmers in one region of the country have an overly wet fall and a particularly harsh winter, they may have very low crop yields for the year. Just a wet fall or just a harsh winter might not have caused such low yields. But together, these two factors caused serious problems for the farmers. Partial cause may be indicated by phrases such as those found in **Table 5-4.**

As an additional exercise, have students write sentences describing things that have happened to them that had partial causes. Students should use as many of the phrases from Table 5-4 as possible. Then have students rewrite their sentences assigning degrees of influence to their causes.

TABLE 5-4 PARTIAL CAUSE

Phrase	Example
a partial cause	Burning of fossil fuels is *a partial cause* of global warming.
is partially responsible for	The advent of better medicines to treat diseases *is partially responsible for* the increase in the average human life span.
a (one) factor is	Genetics is *a factor* in what people look like.
one cause/effect/result is	*One result* of photosynthesis is that plants make their own food.

Students should try to use the words in Table 5-5. However, coming up with other ways of stating partial cause and degree of influence should also be encouraged.

If there are multiple causes or partial causes, the **degree of influence** becomes important. The degree of influence indicates how important or influential a cause is. The author of your science book may want to impress on you how important or influential a particular cause may be. To do so, he or she may use a word of degree. These words are almost always descriptive words and are usually adjectives or adverbs. **Table 5-5** lists some words or phrases that indicate degrees of influence. The table also gives examples of how they are used.

TABLE 5-5 DEGREES OF INFLUENCE

Word or phrase	Example
chiefly	Circulation of atmosphere results *chiefly* from the distribution of solar energy.
greatly	Earth's rotation *greatly* influences all movements of air.
govern	Movements of air *govern* the precipitation of moisture.
an important factor	Genetic mutation is *an important factor* in evolution.
a major influence	Use of automobiles has *a major influence* on air quality.
a minor cause	Liver disease is *a minor cause* of death in the United States today.
a crucial element	Cost reduction is *a crucial element* in making solar power a widely available energy source.

Section 5-2 Cause-and-Effect Patterns, continued

Exercise 4 gives you practice identifying partial cause-and-effect patterns. It also helps you recognize degree-of-influence markers.

Exercise 4 Partial Cause-and-Effect Relationships and their Degrees of Influence

Point out that not all of the partial cause-and-effect relationships will have markers for degree of influence. Also point out that multiple causes can also be partial causes if all of the causes together produce the outcome. This passage is available on **Transparency 29.** Use colored pens to indicate the different types of cause-and-effect markers in the passage.

Read the following passage. As you do, look for the partial cause-and-effect relationships. Then write down the formulas describing them. Also write down, in the space provided, any markers that identify the degree of influence of a partial cause.

The Winds and the Waves

The wind belts, Earth's rotation, and the location of continents are the three factors that control the surface currents of the oceans. The trade winds and the westerlies are the global wind belts that most directly affect the flow of surface currents.

The Coriolis effect is also a major factor controlling surface currents. The Coriolis effect is the deflection of winds and ocean currents caused by Earth's rotation. As a result of the wind belts and the Coriolis effect, huge circles of moving water, called gyres, are formed.

The continents are the third major factor in ocean currents. Continents are obvious barriers to the surface currents. When an ocean surface current flows against a landmass, the current is deflected and divided.

The most important current in the North Atlantic area is called the Gulf Stream. As it moves northeast, it picks up the cold water of the Labrador Current. The Gulf Stream and the Labrador Current together often result in a dense fog in that part of the world. South of Greenland, the Gulf Stream widens and decreases in speed until it becomes the North Atlantic Drift. A drift is a weak current.

(from Modern Earth Science)

a. wind belts + Earth's rotation + location of the continents → surface currents of the oceans

degree of influence markers: _____

b. trade winds + westerlies → flow of surface currents

_____

degree of influence markers: most directly

Section 5-2 Cause-and-Effect Patterns, continued

c. the Coriolis effect → surface currents

_____

degree of influence markers: also a major factor

d. wind belts + Coriolis effect → huge circles of moving water, called gyres

degree of influence markers: _____

e. the continents → ocean surface currents

_____

degree of influence markers: the third major factor

f. Gulf Stream moves northeast + cold Laborador Current → dense fog

_____

degree of influence markers: _____

g. Gulf Stream widens + Gulf Stream decreases speed → North Atlantic drift

degree of influence markers: _____

Probability

When an author is not completely certain of a cause, he or she may indicate this uncertainty in his or her statement. For example, an author might state that *it is possible* that the mass extinction of the dinosaurs was caused by major climatic changes accompanying a collision between a giant meteorite and Earth. The author is not directly stating the cause of the mass extinction because that cause is not known for certain. Instead, the author is proposing a probable cause. We will study **probability** in detail in Chapter 7, but for now you should recognize words and phrases that indicate probability in cause-and-effect relationships.

Table 5-6 on the following page lists some of these markers and gives examples of how they might appear in cause-and-effect descriptions.

_____

Section 5-2 Cause-and-Effect Patterns, continued

_____

TABLE 5-6 WORDS OR PHRASES USED TO INDICATE PROBABILITY

Phrase	Example
in all likelihood	*In all likelihood,* the dinosaurs would not have become extinct without some major global change.
probably	Most meteorites *probably* come from the broken bits of former planets.
there is a strong possibility	*There is a strong possibility* that their disappearance was due to a giant meteor that struck Earth about 65 million years ago.
is/are thought to have	Almost all meteorites *are thought to have* originated within the solar system.
may/may have	Dinosaurs *may have* died out as a result of changes in climate.
possibly	A global catastrophe, such as the extinction of the dinosaurs, *could possibly* be caused by the impact of a large meteor.

Exercise 5   **How Likely Is It?**

Ask students to identify the words or phrases in the probable statements that identified them as probabilities.

a. biologists think (they do not know)

b. may have

c. in all likelihood

d. are thought

For each pair of statements, indicate the number of the statement that demonstrates a probable cause rather than a definite cause.

a. 1_____
   1. Biologists think that small, insect-eating mammals were the ancestors of the first primates, the mammalian group that includes monkeys, apes, and humans.
   2. Several methods of radiometric dating have determined that Earth is approximately 4.5 billion years old.

b. 2_____
   1. A supernova is the death of a large star by explosion.
   2. The universe may have begun with a massive explosion called the big bang.

c. 2_____
   1. The most recent ice age began more than 2 million years ago. Its massive ice sheets started to retreat only 18,000 years ago.
   2. In all likelihood, Earth will continue to experience ice ages periodically.

d. 1_____
   1. Electrons are thought to move around the nucleus in an electron cloud.
   2. Electrons are negatively charged particles in atoms.

Section 5-2 Cause-and-Effect Patterns, continued

A Series of Cause-and-Effect Relationships

Often in science and other subjects, a series of causes will lead to a certain outcome. For example, in one theory of what happened to the dinosaurs, a meteorite hits Earth and causes a cloud of dust to be kicked up. This cloud of dust then blocks the sun's energy from getting to Earth. The lack of solar energy causes the temperature on the surface of Earth to decrease. The decrease in temperature causes the dinosaurs to die out. This series has four steps to get to the final result. The formula for this series would look like the following:

meteorite hits Earth → cloud of dust → sun's energy
blocked → temperature decreases → dinosaurs die out

A cause-and-effect series can be fairly easy to identify, depending on the kinds of markers the author uses. Regular cause-and-effect markers make this pattern easy to spot. Special markers can make the relationship harder to identify and understand.

Exercise 6   Cause-and-Effect Series

Read the following passage, and write the formulas representing the cause-and-effect series sentences.

What Causes Earthquakes?

As tectonic plates push, pull, or scrape against each other, stress builds up along faults near the plates' edges. In response to this stress, rock in the plates deforms. One type of deformation is called elastic deformation.

Elastic deformation leads to earthquakes. While rock can stretch farther than steel without breaking, it will break at some point. Think of elastically deformed rock as a stretched rubber band. You can stretch a rubber band only so far before it breaks. When the rubber band breaks, it releases energy and the broken pieces return to their unstretched shape.

Like the return of the broken rubber-band pieces to their unstretched shape, elastic rebound is the sudden return of elastically deformed rock to its undeformed shape. When more stress is applied to rock than the rock can withstand, elastic rebound occurs. During elastic rebound, rock releases energy that causes an earthquake.

(from Holt Science and Technology: Earth Science)

a. <u>tectonic plates push + pull + scrape → stress along plates' edges →</u>

<u>rock deforms</u>

Students' answers may vary slightly. The distinction between multiple causes or effects and a series can be very small. For example, some students might consider the response in item (c) to be one long series: *more stress is applied than rock can withstand → elastic rebound → rock releases energy → earthquake.* This response could also be considered correct.

Discuss with the students the other types of cause-and-effect relationships found in the passage after they have had ample opportunity to write down the formulas describing the cause-and-effect series.

a. multiple causes, special markers

b. multiple effects, special markers

c. multiple causes/effects, special markers

Section 5-2 Cause-and-Effect Patterns, continued

b. stretch a rubber band → rubber band breaks → releases energy +

broken pieces return to unstretched shape

c. more stress is applied than rock can withstand → elastic rebound +

rock releases energy → earthquake

Inverted Patterns

The word *inverted* means "reversed in position". You can infer from this information that inverted cause-and-effect relationships have the cause and effect reversed in position. In an **inverted pattern,** the effect (or result) appears *before* the cause in the sentence. In other words, the cause appears *after* the effect. The following paragraph was taken from Exercise 6. Some of the sentences have been altered so that the cause-and-effect patterns have been inverted. Sentences with inverted patterns are boldfaced so that you can easily identify them.

Earthquakes are caused by elastic deformation. While rock can stretch farther than steel without breaking, it will break at some point. Think of elastically deformed rock as a stretched rubber band. You can stretch a rubber band only so far before it breaks. **Energy is released when the rubber band breaks,** and the broken pieces return to their unstretched shape.

Inverted patterns may be indicated by regular cause-and-effect markers or by special markers. **Table 5-7** gives examples of words and patterns that indicate inverted cause-and-effect relationships.

TABLE 5-7 INVERTED PATTERNS

Indicated by regular markers	Indicated by special markers
A is caused by B.	A is a direct reflection of B.
A is a result of B.	A is created by B.
A is due to B.	A is controlled by B.
A results from B.	A is governed by B.
A is influenced by B.	A is changed by B.
A is affected by B.	A originated from B.
A happens as a result of B.	

Read the passage on the following page and note the inverted cause-and-effect patterns. Also notice some of the other patterns we have been studying, such as cause-and-effect series, multiple causes and effects, and any special cause-and-effect markers.

Section 5-2 Cause-and-Effect Patterns, continued

A Star Is Born

The passage is available on **Transparency 30.** Use colored pens to highlight the different types of cause-and-effect patterns found in the passage.

As an additional exercise, have students write down formulas for each inverted cause-and-effect pattern in the passage. These formulas will show a reversed arrow, ←.

The analysis of this passage is as follows:

explosion from nearby star → force on nebula → particles compressed → nebula contracts

gravity → nebula continues to shrink → nebula spins more rapidly

spins faster ← skater pulls arms in close

protostar heats up ← collision + pressure

nebula shrink + gravity pulls matter toward center → pressure in core increases

materials become warmer ← compression

Students can also use Exercise 7 to practice identifying special markers. Ask students to name the letters of those sentences that use special cause-and-effect markers. Sentences (b), (d), (e), and (g) use special markers to describe the cause-and-effect pattern.

A star begins as a nebula, a cloud of gas and dust. The particles in a nebula are held together loosely. When an explosion from a nearby star puts force on the nebula, some of the particles are compressed and the nebula begins to contract.

Gravity causes the nebula to continue to shrink. As the nebula becomes smaller, it begins to spin more rapidly. You may have seen the effect of decreasing diameter on the speed of a spinning object, such as an ice skater. The rate of spin increases as a spinning skater pulls his or her arms in closer to the body.

The shrinking, spinning nebula begins to flatten into a disk of matter with a central core called a protostar. That protostar begins to heat up as a result of two factors. One factor is collision. As the particles move together, they collide and produce heat energy. The other factor is pressure. As the nebula shrinks and the force of gravity pulls matter toward its center, the pressure in the core increases. All materials become warmer when compressed.

(from Modern Earth Science)

Exercise 7   **The Direction of Cause-and-Effect Relationships**

Read each of the following cause-and-effect sentences, and decide whether they are written in the regular direction or in the inverted direction. Write "regular" or "inverted" in the space provided.

a. The major ocean currents result from the distribution of solar heat.

    inverted

b. The friction of the wind creates surface currents on the ocean.

    regular

c. The equatorial currents are due to the trade winds.

    inverted

d. The Gulf Stream is responsible for the mild weather of England.

    regular

e. Rain and snow are governed by the movement of air.

    inverted

_____

Section 5-2 Cause-and-Effect Patterns, continued

_____

f. The arrangement of land masses affects precipitation.

<u>regular</u>

g. In general, precipitation is heavy where air flows upward.

<u>inverted</u>

Exercise 8   **From Regular to Inverted Patterns**

You may wish to point out that as the sentences change from regular cause-and-effect patterns to inverted cause-and-effect patterns, they generally change from being active sentences to being passive sentences.

The following sentences are written as regular cause-and-effect patterns. Rewrite the sentences to form inverted cause-and-effect patterns. The first item is done for you as an example.

a. Air flowing towards the equator causes the trade winds.

The trade winds are caused by air flowing towards the equator.

_____

b. The resistance of prevailing winds creates most surface currents in the ocean.

Most surface currents in the ocean are created by the resistance of

prevailing winds.

c. The trade winds generate broad currents at the equator.

The broad currents at the equator are generated by the trade winds.

_____

d. Earth's rotation greatly influences all movements of air.

All movements of air are greatly influenced by Earth's rotation.

_____

e. Movements of air govern the precipitation of moisture.

The precipitation of moisture is governed by the movements of air.

_____

f. The Gulf Stream is responsible for the mild weather of England.

The mild weather of England is caused by the Gulf Stream.

_____

_____

Section 5-2 Cause-and-Effect Patterns, continued
_____

g. The heat of the equator causes air to rise.

Rising air at the equator is caused by heat.
_____

_____

h. The Coriolis effect produces a change in direction of the trade winds.

A change in the direction of the trade winds is produced by the
_____

Coriolis effect.
_____

i. Contracting clouds of gas probably created the sun and the planets.

The sun and the planets were probably created by contracting clouds
_____

of gas.
_____

Exercise 9 **Identifying Inverted Patterns**

Take a look at the following passage. Use the spaces below and on the next page to write formulas for all of the cause-and-effect patterns in the passage. Be sure to include the directional arrows to indicate which sentences contain inverted patterns.

Flashlights

A typical flashlight has two batteries in it. The batteries each have a positive terminal (marked with a +) and a negative terminal (marked with a −). Both terminals have electrons in them, but there is a greater electron density at the negative terminal. Think of the greater density as being caused by "electrical pressure" inside the battery pushing electrons away from the positive terminal and into the negative terminal.

When you turn on the flashlight, you create a continuous path for the electrons to flow through. The electrons at the negative terminal flow through the metal circuit to the positive terminal because of their higher "pressure." While they are flowing from negative to positive, the electrons pass through the filament in the light bulb, heating the filament and causing it to glow. You break the metallic path and electron flow is prevented when you turn off the flashlight.

(from Holt Chemistry Visualizing Matter)

a. greater electron density ← "electrical pressure" inside the battery
_____

_____

Section 5-2 Cause-and-Effect Patterns, continued

b. electrical pressure → electrons pushed from positive terminal into
   negative terminal
   _____

c. turning on flashlight → continuous path for electrons to flow
   _____

   _____

d. electrons at the negative terminal flow through the metal circuit to
   the positive terminal ← higher "pressure"
   _____

e. electrons pass through filament in light bulb → heat filament +
   filament glows
   _____

f. metallic path broken + electron flow prevented ← turn off the
   flashlight
   _____

Summary of All Cause-and-Effect Patterns

This chapter has covered many different types of cause-and-effect patterns. It may be difficult to sort out all of them in your mind. **Table 5-8** summarizes all of the cause-and-effect patterns that you have studied in this chapter. Exercises 10 through 12 will give you practice identifying and writing each of these patterns.

TABLE 5-8 CAUSE-AND-EFFECT PATTERNS

Pattern	Example
Regular marker	The seasonal distribution of rain *causes* streams to rise.
Special marker	The Gulf Stream *is responsible for* the warmth of the British Isles.
Multiple causes	Patterns of vegetation *and* action of wind account for the movement of earth and sand in desert regions.
Multiple effects	Convection (warm, rising air) is responsible for high winds *and* much of the rain in desert regions.
Partial cause	Burning of fossil fuels *is a partial cause* of global warming.
Degree of influence	The distribution of solar energy *chiefly* results in the circulation of the atmosphere.
Probability	A global catastrophe, such as the extinction of the dinosaurs, could *possibly* be caused by the impact of a large meteor.
Series	In the region of the equator, the air rises and *thus* becomes cool. *As a result,* the equatorial regions generally get heavy rainfall.
Inverted	The major ocean currents *result from* the distribution of solar heat.

Section 5-2 Cause-and-Effect Patterns, continued

Exercise 10   Cause-and-Effect Patterns

This passage is available on **Transparency 31.** Use colored pens to highlight the different types of cause-and-effect patterns.

Read the following passage on the formation of minerals. Then write down the formulas for the different kinds of cause-and-effect sentences. Label each formula with the type of cause-and-effect pattern or patterns.

Formation of Minerals

Changing conditions beneath Earth's surface can alter the mineral composition of a preexisting rock. When changes in pressure, temperature, or chemical makeup alter a rock, metamorphism takes place. Minerals that form in metamorphic rock include calcite, garnet, graphite, hematite, magnetite, mica, and talc.

A hot, liquid solution is formed when ground water, heated by magma, works its way through cracks in overlying rock and reacts with minerals in the walls of the cracks. Dissolved metals and other elements crystallize out of the hot fluid to form new minerals. Gold, copper, sulfur, pyrite, and galena form in such hot-water environments.

As magma moves upward, it fills in pockets in preexisting rock, forming small, teardrop-shaped formations called pegmatites. Minerals crystallize from this magma as it cools. The presence of hot fluids causes the mineral crystals to become extremely large, sometimes growing to several meters across! Many gems and rare minerals such as topaz and tourmaline form in pegmatites.

(from Holt Science and Technology: Earth Science)

a. changing conditions beneath Earth's surface → altered mineral

composition of preexisting rock

pattern or patterns probability, special markers

b. changes in pressure + changes in temperature + changes in chemical

makeup → altered rock → metamorphism

pattern or patterns multiple causes, series, special markers

c. hot, liquid solution ← ground water heated by magma + minerals in

the walls of cracks

pattern or patterns inverted, multiple cause, special markers

Section 5-2 Cause-and-Effect Patterns, continued

d. dissolved metals from hot fluid + other elements from hot fluid →
new minerals

pattern or patterns _multiple causes, special markers_

e. magma moves upward → fills in pockets in preexisting rock → small
teardrop-shaped formations called pegmatites

pattern or patterns _series, special markers_

f. minerals crystallize ← magma cools

pattern or patterns _inverted with special marker_

g. hot fluids → mineral crystals become extremely large

pattern or patterns _regular marker_

Exercise 11   Cause-and-Effect Directions

This exercise is intended for students to find whether they fully understand the meanings of the cause-and-effect relationships in the passage. If they can identify the direction of the pattern even when that direction is taken out of context, then they should have a good understanding of the cause-and-effect relationship.

Reread the passage in Exercise 10. Then, without looking back, see if you can draw the appropriate arrow (→ or ←) to indicate the correct cause-and-effect relationships between the items listed below. The relationships below are not necessarily in the same direction as the relationships in the passage.

a. new minerals _____←_____ dissolved metals from hot liquid + other elements from hot liquid

b. a hot, liquid solution _____←_____ ground water heated by magma + minerals

c. magma cools _____→_____ minerals crystallize

d. the presence of hot fluids _____→_____ mineral crystals become extremely large

e. changes in temperature + pressure + chemical makeup _____→_____ metamorphism

f. teardrop-shaped formations _____←_____ magma fills in pockets in preexisiting rock

Section 5-2 Cause-and-Effect Patterns, continued

Exercise 12 **Writing Cause-and-Effect Patterns**

Students' answers will vary. The answers given here are examples of correct answers. Make sure students attempt to use each applicable pattern. This exercise could be done by student pairs. Assign each team of students a cause-and-effect pair. Ask them to write cause-and-effect sentences using as many different patterns as they can. Have all teams present their work by recording their patterns on the board.

Using the cause-and-effect patterns in Table 5-8, write sentences with the pairs of cause and effect below. Use as many different patterns as you can. The first item is done for you as an example.

Cause	**Effect**
a. Air is hot near the equator.	It rises.

Because air near the equator is hot, it rises.

_____

| **b.** The atmosphere is thinnest around 0° latitude. | The air around the equator is very hot. |

The air around the equator is very hot because the atmosphere is

thinnest around 0° latitude.

| **c.** The mild Gulf Stream flows northeast past Norway. | Norway remains ice-free all year round. |

The mild Gulf Stream flows northeast past Norway and keeps the

country ice-free year round.

| **d.** The Gulf Stream picks up the cold Labrador Current. | Dense fog occurs in that part of the world. |

As a result of the Gulf Stream picking up the cold Labrador Current,

dense fog occurs in that part of the world.

| **e.** There is very little rainfall between 20° and 30° latitude. | Most deserts are found in this region. |

Because of the lack of rainfall between 20° and 30° latitude, most

deserts are found in this region.

| **f.** In deserts, the warm air rises (convection). | Deserts have high winds. |

The high winds of the desert are a result of convection.

_____

Section 5-2 Cause-and-Effect Patterns, continued

g. Deserts have warm air.   Deserts have greater evaporation.

The warm air in deserts results in greater evaporation.

_____

h. Water evaporates quickly.   There is little left for grass and bushes.

The quick evaporation of water means there is little water left for

grass and bushes.

i. There is dry climate.   There is little vegetation in deserts.

Dry climate is responsible for the lack of vegetation in deserts.

_____

j. Air around the equator rises.   It becomes cool.

As air around the equator rises, it becomes cool.

_____

GLOSSARY

degree of influence a word or phrase that indicates how important or influential a cause is (79)

inverted pattern a pattern in which the effect appears before the cause in the sentence (84)

partial cause one of several causes of an event (79)

probability something that is a possible cause or outcome but is not a definite cause or outcome (81)

regular cause-and-effect marker a word or phrase that normally marks a cause-and-effect relationship (72)

special cause-and-effect marker a word or phrase that can be used to mark a cause-and-effect relationship but can have other functions as well (74)

6-1 How We Compare Things

As an introduction to the chapter, ask students to describe the importance of making comparisons in their daily lives and in scientific discourse. Ask them to find one example of a statement of comparison or contrast from the chapter of their science book that they are currently studying.

One of the most important ways we understand things is by comparing them to other things. How can you say that something is big or expensive unless you have some feeling for what big or expensive means. How big? How expensive? What if you describe someone as friendly or happy? Friendly and happy only have meaning when compared to unfriendly and sad.

Comparisons give meaning to descriptions. You could say that a particular hat is inexpensive, but do you mean that it costs 5 cents or $50? If you say the hat is as inexpensive as a gallon of gasoline, you have a better idea of the hat's cost. The hat has been compared to a gallon of gasoline.

The skill of comparing is important whether you are in or out of school, no matter what you are dealing with—people, studies, or any big decisions you have to make. When you have an important decision to make, comparing the situation to a past experience can make your decision easier. The goal of this chapter is to help you develop your ability to make and understand comparisons, especially in the field of science.

To compare two things, those things must have some relationship to each other, or something in common. You may have heard the phrase, "They are as different as apples and oranges." But apples and oranges are related because they are both fruits. Or you may have heard, "They are as different as night and day." But night and day are related. They are both times of the day. Both of these examples use a comparison to describe people that are different.

Basically, there are two ways to compare things. Things are either alike or they are different. The term **contrast** is used to describe the process of comparing two things that are different. The two sentences in the previous paragraph are examples of contrast. When things are different, they usually differ in one of two ways: the first item is either less than or greater than the item it is being contrasted against. The following sentences demonstrate a "less than" comparison and a "greater than" comparison respectively.

There is less rain at 50° north latitude than at the equator.
The polar region is colder than the equator.

Things can also be alike in two ways: they can be similar or the same. Notice the comparisons in the following examples. The first sentence is an example of a similarity. The likeness in the second sentence is an example of sameness.

The climates between 20° and 30° north latitude and 20° and 30° south latitude are *similar*.

The populations of France and Italy are roughly the *same*.

Section 6-1 How We Compare Things, continued

Exercise 1 Identifying Comparisons

Decide which sentences compare or contrast and what kind of comparison they are (less, greater, similar, or the same).

For Peat's Sake

[a] The partial decomposition of plant remains produces a brownish-black material called peat. [b] Over time, peat deposits are covered by layers of sediments. [c] The weight of these overlying sediments squeezes out water and gas from the peat. [d] It then becomes a denser material called lignite, or brown coal.

[e] The pressure of more deposited sediments further compresses the lignite and forms bituminous coal, or soft coal. [f] Bituminous coal is the most abundant type of coal. [g] Where the folding of Earth's crust produces extremely high temperatures and pressure, bituminous coal is changed into anthracite, the hardest form of coal. [h] Bituminous coal and anthracite consist of 80 to 90 percent carbon and produce a great amount of heat when they burn.

(from Modern Earth Science)

a. not a comparison _____

b. not a comparison _____

c. not a comparison _____

d. greater than _____

e. greater than _____

f. greater than _____

g. greater than _____

h. the same _____

Exercise 2 Similar or Different?

Decide if these pairs are similar or different. Compare or contrast the two items with a sentence using the word or words in parentheses as a basis of comparison. The first item is done for you as an example.

a. humus/topsoil (rich)

Humus is richer than topsoil. _____

This passage is available on **Transparency 32.** Team students in groups of two or three. Ask each group to examine one sentence of the passage. Using the transparency, require each team to elect a spokesperson to report and justify their work. Have the groups explain how they arrived at their answers.

d. It then becomes a <u>denser</u> material.

e. The pressure of <u>more</u> deposited sediments <u>further compresses</u> the lignite.

f. Bituminous coal is <u>the most abundant</u> type of coal.

g. anthracite, the <u>hardest</u> form of coal

h. Bituminous coal <u>and</u> anthracite consist of 80 to 90 percent carbon

See if students can use their own points of comparison to come up with other comparisons for the two items in each part of Exercise 2.

Section 6-1 How We Compare Things, continued

b. platinum/bronze (cost)

Platinum is much more expensive than bronze.

c. iron/silver (metal versus nonmetal)

Both iron and silver are metals.

d. emeralds/rubies (type of stone)

Emeralds and rubies are expensive gemstones.

e. soy sauce/tofu (source)

Soy sauce and tofu are made from soybeans.

f. dinosaurs/crocodiles (class)

Dinosaurs and crocodiles are reptiles.

g. monkeys/gorillas (size)

Monkeys are smaller than gorillas.

h. fossil fuels/solar power (pollution, cost)

Fossil fuels pollute more than solar power does, but they are less

expensive.

i. nuclear power/wind power (danger, cost)

Nuclear power is more dangerous than wind power. It is also much

less expensive.

Section 6-1 How We Compare Things, continued

    j. rain forests/other types of forests (variety of plants and animals)

      Rain forests have a greater variety of plants and animals than any

      other types of forests do.

    k. coniferous forests/rain forests (rainfall)

      Coniferous forests get a lot less rainfall than rain forests do.

Features

When we contrast things, we compare their different **features.** Think about Exercise 2. The bases of comparison given in parentheses are features of the two items. These features are used to compare or contrast them. **Table 6-1** uses examples from Exercise 2 to point out features used to compare or contrast the pairs.

TABLE 6-1 FEATURES OF COMPARISON

Pair	Sentence	Feature
Platinum/bronze	Platinum is more expensive than bronze.	cost
Soy sauce/tofu	Soy sauce and tofu are made from soybeans.	origin
Nuclear power/ wind power	Nuclear power is more dangerous than wind power.	danger
Coniferous forest/ rain forest	Coniferous forests have less rainfall than rain forests do.	rainfall

    The features used to compare two items will depend on the topic you are studying. For example, try contrasting dolphins and rainbow trout. If you are studying ecosystems, you could compare them based on the feature of where they live. Dolphins live in the ocean. Rainbow trout generally live in streams and lakes. If you want to know more about their appearance, you could compare them based on size. Dolphins are much larger than rainbow trout. If you are studying the classification of animals, you could compare them based on class. Dolphins are mammals; rainbow trout are fish. Each of these contrasts is equally correct. Which feature you choose depends on what is important to you at that time.

Section 6-1 How We Compare Things, continued

Exercise 3   Comparing Features

Initiate Exercise 3 using photographs that show a variety of elements. Allow students to make comparisons, and elicit the various features that are discussed in the passage. The features being compared in the passage include the following: physical state, shininess, and malleability. See if students can come up with any other features for comparing or contrasting the three classes of elements. Possibilities include electrical conductivity and reactivity.

Read the following passage. Determine the feature being compared for each pair listed.

The Elements

Elements are classified as metals, nonmetals, and metalloids, according to their properties. Most of the elements in the periodic table are metals. Most metals are solid at room temperature. Mercury, however, is a liquid. More than half of the nonmetals are gases at room temperature. Metalloids are also called semiconductors. Metalloids have some properties of metals and some properties of nonmetals.

Metals tend to be shiny. You can see a reflection in a mirror because light reflects off the shiny surface of a thin layer of silver behind the glass. Sulfur, like most nonmetals, is not shiny.

Most metals are malleable, which means that they can be flattened with a hammer without shattering. Aluminum is flattened into sheets to make cans and foil. Nonmetals are not malleable. In fact, solid nonmetals, such as carbon (the graphite of a pencil lead), are brittle and will break or shatter when hit with a hammer. Tellurium is a metalloid. Like a metal, tellurium is shiny but it is also brittle and is easily smashed into a powder.

(from Holt Science and Technology: Physical Science)

a. most metals/half of the nonmetals

physical state at room temperature

b. silver/sulfur

shininess

c. aluminum/carbon

malleability

d. tellurium/metals

shininess and malleability

6-2 The Role of Comparison

A beach is *also* a sandy region. Have students define a beach (a sandy region that borders a body of water). Students can then contrast a desert with a beach.

Comparison is an important part of other thinking skills that you have studied, including describing, defining, and classifying. A formal definition compares an item to other members of its class. In Chapter 3, for example, a desert was defined as a sandy region with very little water. If a desert were simply defined as a sandy region, the definition would also include other sandy areas such as beaches. By stating that a desert is a sandy region with very little water, the definition contrasts deserts with all other sandy regions. Thus, the definition fits only deserts.

Classifying is also based on comparison. In classifying, one puts things that are similar into the same class. As an example, think about the different kinds of metals. Study the taxonomy shown in **Figure 6-1.** In this classification, metals are divided into three categories, nonprecious pure metals, precious pure metals, and alloys. All of the items in the classification tree are similar because they are all metals. The different classes provide features for comparing the different metals. What makes silver, platinum, and gold similar? What do steel, bronze, and brass have in common? Do you remember the definition of an alloy? Alloys are metals that are a mixture of more than one pure metal. The features used in this tree are composition of the metal and value of the metal.

FIGURE 6-1 Classification trees can give a visual representation of a comparison.

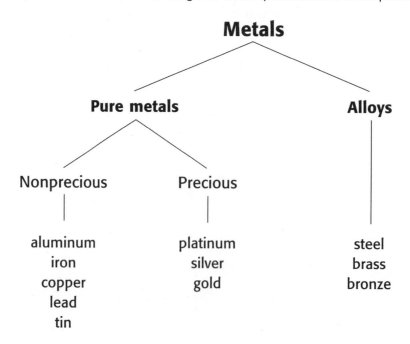

Section 6-2 The Role of Comparison, continued

Exercise 4 **Contrasting Items in the Same Class**

Contrast each of these items with another item in the same class. The first item is done for you as an example.

a. A tiger is a large striped cat found only in Asia. In contrast, *a lion is also a large cat, but it has no stripes.*

b. A plane is a tool used to shave the edges of wood. In contrast, a saw is a tool used to cut wood.

c. A dog is a domestic animal that sometimes guards the home. In contrast, a cat is a domestic animal that rarely serves as a guardian of the home.

d. A bay is a body of water surrounded on three sides by land. In contrast, a lagoon is a body of water surrounded on all sides by land.

e. The liver is an organ that purifies the blood. In contrast, the brain is an organ that controls the nervous system.

f. The circulatory system carries nutrients and oxygen through the body. In contrast, the nervous system carries nerve impulses through the body.

g. The biosphere includes all life on Earth and the physical environment that supports it. In contrast, the hydrosphere includes only the physical environments that contain water.

h. Biology is a science that studies living things. In contrast, earth science covers the study of Earth and the universe around it.

Section 6-2 The Role of Comparison, continued

i. Telephones are instruments that send messages along wires and cables. In contrast, <u>radios are instruments that send messages through the air.</u>

Exercise 5   Analyzing Comparisons

Read the following passage. Decide which sentences contain statements of comparison or contrast and what kind of comparison they are (different, less than, greater than, or similar). Some sentences may contain more than one type of comparison.

This passage is available on **Transparency 33.** Use different-colored pens to highlight the different types of comparisons. Lead a discussion so that students understand the following comparisons.

a. Earlier life-forms were simpler than organisms today.

c. The ancient horse is similar in size to a dog. The ancient horse differs from the modern horse in the number of toes on its front feet.

e. Penguins, alligators, bats, and people are similar in that they all have backbones.

f. These vertebrates have similar bones in their front limbs.

g. The functions of the front limbs of penguins, alligators, bats, and people are different.

h. Vertebrates might have come from the same ancestor.

Fossils and Evolution

[a] According to biologists, all organisms living today evolved from earlier, simpler life-forms. [b] The modern horse, for example, evolved from an ancestor that existed 50 million years ago. [c] The earlier relative was the size of a dog and had four toes on its front foot; its modern version has only one.

[d] Animals with backbones are called vertebrates. [e] Penguins, alligators, bats, and humans all have backbones and are thus considered vertebrates. [f] The front limbs (known as forelimbs) of all these vertebrates have similar sets of bones. [g] The functions of these structures have evolved into different uses. [h] And yet the similarity in the structure of these bones can still be seen, which suggests that all vertebrates share a common ancestor.

(from Biology Principles and Explorations)

a. <u>less than</u>

b. <u>not a comparison</u>

c. <u>similar (size) and greater than (number of toes)</u>

d. <u>not a comparison</u>

e. <u>similar</u>

f. <u>similar</u>

g. <u>different</u>

h. <u>similar</u>

Section 6-2 The Role of Comparison, continued

Comparison Tables

Before students have had a chance to see Table 6-2, draw a blank table, on the board, that includes the first row and first column. Ask students to fill in the table using the information in the passage for Exercise 1. After students have completed their tables, explain that they have just created a comparison table. Allow them to look at Table 6-2 and compare it to their own. The passage is available on **Transparency 32.**

Most reading passages will make many comparisons of many different items. It can be quite difficult to keep all of these comparisons straight in your mind as you read the passage. If you do not find a way to organize the many comparisons a passage may contain, you will have great difficulty understanding the passage.

When a textbook is making several comparisons, one of the best ways to understand them is to draw a **comparison table.** A comparison table, as its name suggests, is a table that lists the different items being compared and the features that are used to compare them. When creating a comparison table, put the items being compared in the first column and put the features in the first row.

Look back at the passage "For Peat's Sake" from Section 6-1 on page 94. This passage contains comparisons of four different materials that all derive from the decomposition of plant remains. Exercise 1 asked you to examine these comparisons sentence by sentence. This way, it is easy to see how peat compares to lignite, or how bituminous coal compares to anthracite. But there are no sentences directly comparing peat to anthracite, or lignite to anthracite. A comparison table helps you see how all four of the decomposition products compare to one another. The table gives you a better understanding of the material in the text. A comparison table of the information in this passage might look like **Table 6-2.**

TABLE 6-2 COMPARISON TABLE OF COAL TYPES

| Item | Feature | | | |
	Hardness/Density	Formation	% Carbon	Heat Production
Peat	lightest	decomposition of plants		
Lignite	denser than peat	compression of peat		
Bituminous coal	denser than lignite	compression of lignite	80–90%	high
Anthracite	hardest	high temperature and pressure from folding of Earth's crust	80–90%	high

Section 6-2 The Role of Comparison, continued

Exercise 6   **Writing Comparisons from a Comparison Table**

Without using numbers, write a paragraph making some general comparisons between the three small celestial bodies described in the comparison table below.

	Size	Orbit	Composition	Origin
Comet	0.5 km to 100 km in diameter tail can be millions of kilometers long	orbits sun	ice rock cosmic dust	leftover from the process of planet formation
Asteroid	few meters to 900 km in diameter	orbits sun	rock some contain organic material some contain metals	leftover from formation of solar system
Meteoroid	smaller than asteroid	orbits sun	rock some contain organic material some contain metals	probably from asteroids

Asteroids can be the largest of the small celestial bodies. Meteoroids are the smallest. Comets can be larger than asteroids, but not all are. They can also have tails that are much larger than any other small celestial body. All three small celestial bodies orbit the sun. All three of the celestial bodies contain rock. Comets also contain ice. Asteroids and meteoroids can contain organic matter or metals. Both comets and asteroids originated as leftovers when the solar system formed. Meteoroids probably originated from asteroids.

CHAPTER

6 COMPARISON

6-3 The Language of Comparison

As an introduction to this lesson, ask students to brainstorm lists of comparison words. Have them think about words they use everyday to indicate similarity or difference. Ask them to think of words that might be found in a science textbook to indicate similarity or difference. Point out that these two sets of words will overlap significantly.

There is a whole *language* of comparison. This language is made up of **comparison words.** Comparison words are words that indicate a statement of comparison or contrast. The sentence *Five is greater than four* shows a simple example of how comparison words are used. The words *greater than* tell you that the numbers are being contrasted against one another.

Think back to Chapter 1 on descriptions. One way to describe an object was to compare it to another, more familiar object. Most of the time these descriptions were written as similarities rather than differences. Many comparison words are used to compare two similar, or like, things. **Table 6-3** lists a few comparison words used to describe likeness and gives examples of how they are used

TABLE 6-3 COMPARISON WORDS USED TO INDICATE LIKENESS

Word or phrase	Example
the same as	A meteorite is the same as a meteoroid that has entered Earth's atmosphere.
as heavy as	One atom of helium is as heavy as two atoms of hydrogen.
the same shape as	A florence flask has the same shape as a pear.
are basically the same as	Savannas are basically the same as tropical grasslands with scattered trees and shrubs.
are similar/alike	The shape of DNA is similar to a very long microscopic ladder that has been twisted.
-like	Pterodactyls were birdlike reptiles that lived 150 million years ago.

Sometimes statements of comparison are based on two items being different. These types of statements—statements of contrast—have their own comparison words. Many of these comparison words are adjectives with suffixes that indicate degree. For example, the adjective *large* can be turned into a comparison word by adding either the suffix *-er* to make *larger* or the suffix *-est* to make *largest*. **Table 6-4,** on the following page, lists some of the words, phrases, and suffixes used to express difference. The table also gives examples of the kinds of sentences in which these words might be found.

Section 6-3 The Language of Comparison, continued

TABLE 6-4 COMPARISON WORDS USED TO INDICATE DIFFERENCE

Word, phrase, or suffix	Example
-er than	Anthracite is denser than lignite.
more than	Platinum is more expensive than gold.
less than	Silver is less expensive than gold.
-est	Pluto is the coldest planet.
compare/compared to	Jupiter is a huge planet when compared to Earth.
contrast/in contrast to	Deciduous trees lose their leaves in the fall in contrast to evergreen trees, which do not.
differ/differentiate	Metamorphic, igneous, and sedimentary rock differ in how they form.
distinct/distinguish	Electrical conductivity can be used to distinguish the metals from the nonmetals.
as opposed to	Biology is the study of living things as opposed to geology, which is the study of Earth and its rocks.
on the other hand	Farmers can be devastated by flood. On the other hand, drought can be equally disastrous.
unlike	Cheetahs are extremely fast runners, unlike turtles, which move very slowly.

Exercise 7 Comparison Words

Read the passage and list all the words that are used for comparisons. There may be more lines than you need.

Stars and Our Star

Life on Earth is dependent upon the sun, the star nearest Earth. Except for its relationship to Earth, the sun is similar to billions of other stars. From Earth, most stars in the night sky appear to be tiny specks of white light. However, if you look closely at the stars, you will notice that they vary in color.

Section 6-3 The Language of Comparison, continued

This passage is available on **Transparency 34.** Underline the elements of comparison on the transparency as you go over Exercise 7. Guide the class discussion so that the following comparison words are pointed out.

· To *vary* means to differ from.

· In the multiplication sense, *times* is sometimes a comparison word.

· Medium-sized stars are only medium sized in comparison to all other stars.

· Fractions (and percentages) can be comparisons. For example, a nickel is worth 1/2, or 50 percent of a dime.

Stars vary in size and mass as well as in color. Some stars are less than 20 km in diameter, far smaller than Earth. Other stars have a diameter 1,000 times that of the sun. The sun, a medium-sized star, has a diameter of about 1,392,000 km. Most stars that are visible in the night sky are medium-sized stars.

Many stars also have about the same mass as the sun, which is about 330,000 times more massive than Earth. Some small stars have only 1/50 of the sun's mass. Large stars have more than 50 times the sun's mass. Stars also differ in composition, temperature, and brightness.

(from Modern Earth Science)

nearest	medium-sized (used twice)
similar	many
most	about the same
vary (used twice)	about 330,000 times more massive
some	only 1/50
less than	more than 50 times
smaller than	also differ in
other	
1000 times that of	

Exercise 8   Writing Comparisons

How many different ways can you compare the sun and Earth? Write as many sentences of comparison as you can.

The sun is many times larger than Earth. Earth is many times smaller than the sun. The sun is a star; Earth is a planet. The sun is to Earth as Earth is to the moon. The sun is much hotter than Earth. The sun is made of gases, while Earth is made up of many different types of matter.

Students' answers will vary. The answers given here are examples of correct answers. Allow students to work individually as you monitor their progress. If students need help, they may use the words in Tables 6-3 and 6-4 for ideas. Select students to write sentences on the board as they finish.

Section 6-3 The Language of Comparison, continued

Exercise 9   Using Comparison Words

Exercise 9 could be assigned as homework to give students ample time to think of creative statements of comparison and contrast. Students' answers will vary. Encourage students to use as many different types of comparisons as they can. Also encourage them to use a wide variety of comparison words.

What are some ways you can compare yourself to your mother, father, or other relatives? Write 4 sentences comparing and contrasting yourself to an older relative. Use as many comparison words as possible.

a. _____

_____

_____

_____

b. _____

_____

_____

_____

c. _____

_____

_____

_____

d. _____

_____

_____

_____

GLOSSARY

comparison table a table that lists the different items being compared or contrasted and their similarities or differences (101)

comparison words words that indicate a comparison (103)

contrast to compare with respect to differences (93)

feature an aspect used as a basis for comparison (96)

7-1 What Is a Hypothesis?

Ask students how they would test each hypothesis, and record their responses on the board or overhead. Accept all answers. For example: Telephone the power station, look in the kitchen, or look outside the house and see if lights are off in other houses.

A **hypothesis** is a possible explanation of why something may have happened or a prediction of what might happen. It is an explanation of the possible cause of a problem or a possible solution to a problem. For example, imagine that you are sitting at home when suddenly the lights go out. You need to find out why the lights went out, so that you know what to do to get the lights back on. In coming up with possible causes, you are formulating hypotheses. Some of your hypotheses might include the following: a problem with the electric generator at the power station, a break in the electric cable leading to the house, or a circuit overload caused by someone using too many kitchen appliances at one time. Each of these hypotheses can be tested to determine if it is the true cause of why the lights went out.

In order for a predicted solution to be a hypothesis, you must be able to test it. Otherwise, your prediction or solution is merely a guess. The hypothesis is the most important tool of scientific research. Most scientific experiments begin with a hypothesis. Then the experiment or experiments are carried out to test that hypothesis.

As you go through this chapter—and through your science texts—notice the kinds of words that are used with hypotheses. A scientist *formulates* a hypothesis. It is also correct to say that a scientist *states*, *forms*, or *frames* a hypothesis. The hypothesis is tested by observation and experimentation. After the scientist weighs the **evidence,** the hypothesis is *accepted* (proved, verified, or confirmed) or *rejected* (disproved). **Figure 7-1** gives you a visual representation of how hypotheses are used in science.

FIGURE 7-1 The Life of Hypotheses

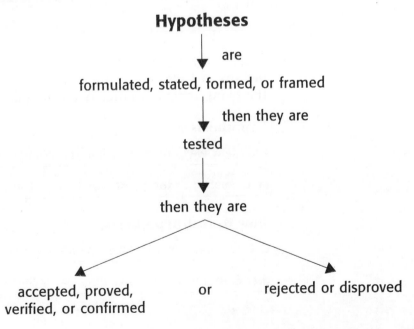

Section 7-1 What Is a Hypothesis?, continued

Exercise 1 **Formulating Hypotheses**

Formulate a hypothesis for each of the following situations. Then decide how to test your hypothesis.

a. You ordered an item by mail. It was supposed to arrive in 2 weeks, but 3 weeks later the package has not arrived. Why?

hypothesis:

The company did not receive the request; the package was lost in the

mail; the item was out of stock; or the company is out of business.

how to test hypothesis:

Telephone the post office or the company.

b. You are supposed to meet a friend for lunch at 1:00 P.M. Your friend has never been to the restaurant, so you wrote out directions for him. By 2:00 P.M. he has not arrived. Why?

hypothesis:

He forgot the appointment; he lost the directions; he had an accident

while he was traveling; or some important problem came up.

how to test hypothesis:

Call your friend.

c. You are trying to grow a plant in your bedroom. The plant looks healthy at first, but in a few days, the leaves turn brown, and the plant appears to die. What happened?

hypothesis:

The plant was not getting enough sunlight; the plant was getting too

much water; or the plant was getting too little water.

how to test hypothesis:

Get two identical plants. Place one where you had placed the plant

that died. Place the other directly by the window.

CHAPTER

7   **HYPOTHESIS, PROBABILITY, AND PREDICTION**

7-2 Observation and Inference

What do you need in order to form a hypothesis? A hypothesis is not just a random guess; it is a prediction based on some facts, or **observations.** You studied the concept of observation in Chapter 1. But a hypothesis is not a proven fact, so it is also based on **inference.** Inference means drawing conclusions about the things you have observed. For example, suppose you hear a crash coming from your bedroom. You enter the room to find your window broken and a baseball rolling across the floor. You can infer that someone hit the baseball through your window and broke it. You did not see the incident happen, but you can make a hypothesis based on your inference.

A very important part of scientific thinking—and thinking in general—is the ability to separate observation and inference. Observations are things you have experienced through the senses, by seeing, hearing, tasting, touching, or smelling. An inference is an explanation or interpretation of what you have observed.

Two people can observe the same situation, and if they are careful observers, they can use their observations to come up with facts about the situation that are not subject to opinion. Inference is very different. Inference depends greatly on personal opinion and ideas. Therefore, two people might observe the exact same events, and infer very different things from them. Hypotheses must be tested. For this reason they are not considered to be fact. If hypotheses were based only on observation and not on inference, there would be no need to test them; they would be fact. Exercise 2 tests your skills in identifying observation and inferences.

Exercise 2   **Observation and Inference**

Read the following passage and decide: (a) what observations Inspector Richards made and (b) what inferences were based on each observation.

Murder?

The rain had just stopped. Inspector Richards arrived at the house at 2 P.M. The front door was locked. He pried open the door and went in. Mrs. Williams was lying in bed. She was dead. The bedroom window faced the garden. The window was open and there were several small puddles of water between Mrs. Williams's bed and the window. The woman was wearing a pearl necklace, and there was a bottle of pills on the night table near the bed. Mr. Williams was out of town on business.

Section 7-2 Observation and Inference, continued

At the conclusion of the exercise, require each student to define, in his or her own words, the terms *observation* and *inference* and to give an example not from this exercise for each.

Because Mrs. Williams was still wearing her pearls, robbery could not have been the motive. It was obviously a case of murder. The murderer must have come in through the bedroom window and killed Mrs. Williams. The puddles of water were probably left by his shoes.

a. Observation

   i. Mrs. Williams was dead

   _____

   ii. Mrs. Williams was wearing pearls.

   _____

   iii. The windows were open.

   _____

   iv. There were several small puddles of water between Mrs.

   Williams's bed and the window.

   _____

b. Inference

   i. Mrs. Williams was murdered.

   _____

   ii. The pearls were valuable. The motive was not robbery.

   _____

   iii. The murderer came in and left through the window.

   _____

   iv. The puddles of water were left by the murderer's shoes.

   _____

CHAPTER

7 HYPOTHESIS, PROBABILITY, AND PREDICTION

7-3 Prediction

Some hypotheses explain why events happened in a certain way. Some hypotheses predict what will happen in the future. These hypotheses tell you how things will *probably* behave in the future. Suppose one student says to another, "If you study hard, you will pass the test." This statement is a **prediction.** For example, some astronomers hypothesize that the solar system will be destroyed in 10 billion years. Others predict that the universe will go on expanding forever.

To make good predictions, scientists begin with evidence that gives some indication of what will happen. For example, astronomers can tell that the universe is currently expanding and that it has been expanding for as long as they can determine. This evidence leads them to predict that the universe might go on expanding forever. Exercise 3 gives you practice looking at evidence and using it to make predictions. Exercises 4 and 5 require that you seek out evidence to make accurate predictions.

Exercise 3 **Making Predictions**

Study the information in the two images below. Think of some primary predictions and their secondary effects; that is, things that may or will happen as a result of other things. You will be asked to make specific predictions based on the information in these images and the other images that follow.

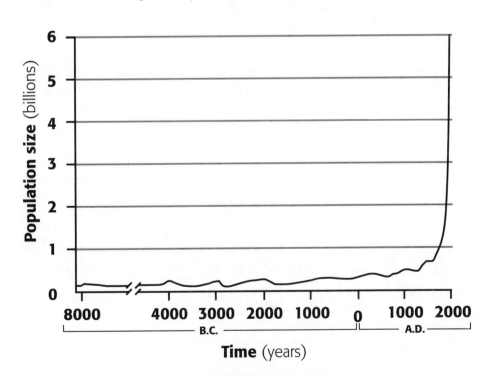

World Population Growth

Section 7-3 Prediction, continued

Introduce this exercise with a variety of prediction statements dealing with the future and the past. Allow students to work in pairs. The pairs should discuss their opinions of what will happen based on the images given. Each student should be able to justify his or her opinions to the partner. It is likely that students' answers will vary. As long as the answers can be supported by the images in the text, they should be accepted.

a. What will happen if the world population continues to grow at its present rate?

The world population is growing at a very rapid rate. If this growth

rate continues, Earth might run out of space for all those people.

Earth would probably not be able to produce enough food and other

necessities for all of the people.

_____

_____

_____

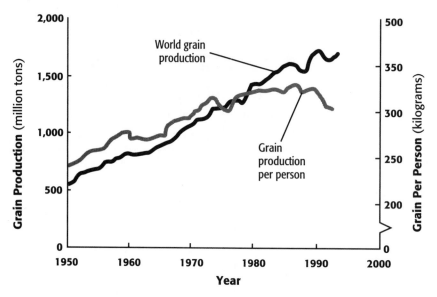

Changes in World Grain Production

b. What do you think will happen if the current trends in both population growth and in grain production continue?

Even though total grain production is increasing, grain production per

person is decreasing. If the world's population grows at its current

rate and grain production per person continues to decrease, the num-

ber of people suffering from famine could increase.

_____

_____

Section 7-3 Prediction, continued

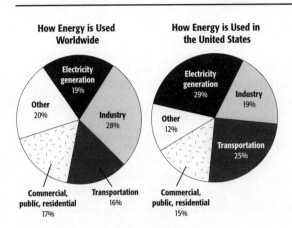

Energy Usage

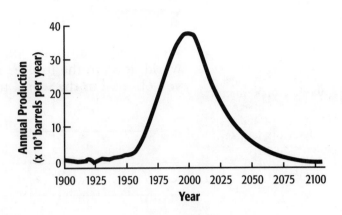

Oil Production

c. If all energy came from oil, which aspect of life in the United States would have the greatest problem in the year 2100? Why?

If all energy came from oil, as oil production decreases, there would be less energy. In the United States, electricity generation uses the most energy. Therefore, if there were less energy available, electricity generation would have the biggest problems.

d. Air pollution threatens the health of all people. The three main sources of air pollution are transportation, burning fuel apart from transportation, and industry. If population growth continues along its current trend without an increase in industrial growth, which source of pollution will become the biggest problem?

Transportation should become the biggest polluter because more people will mean that there is a greater need for transportation. This conclusion assumes no industrial growth.

Section 7-3 Prediction, continued

Exercise 4   **Predicting the World's Future**

Students' answers will vary based on their perceptions of the world around them. You might assign Exercises 4 and 5 as homework to give students plenty of time to come up with thoughtful answers.

What are some things you think might happen that would make world news in the future? Make some predictions based on trends you observe in the world today.

_____

_____

_____

_____

_____

_____

_____

_____

_____

_____

Exercise 5   **Predicting Your Own Future**

Exercise 5 provides a good opportunity for students to examine how current events can affect future ones and how hypotheses help link the two. The last part of this question that asks them the likelihood of their predictions is a good tie-in to Section 7-4 on probability. Use this exercise to introduce Section 7-4.

What will happen to you in the future? Make some predictions about yourself. How likely are your hypotheses to be proven true?

_____

_____

_____

_____

_____

_____

_____

_____

CHAPTER

7 HYPOTHESIS, PROBABILITY, AND PREDICTION

7-4 Probability

Use the probability portion of Exercise 5 to introduce this section. Ask students for some common words and phrases that indicate zero possibility, such as *no way, not,* and *hardly,* etc.

If a friend comes to you and says, "Our science exam is going to be really tough," they have stated a hypothesis. You might respond by saying, "No way!" You have just stated that there is a very low chance, or low probability, that your friend's hypothesis is correct.

In many cases, a hypothesis cannot be proved completely. Think back to Section 7-3, where you read about astronomers' hypothesis that the universe will continue expanding forever. These astronomers cannot see into the future, nor can they live until the end of time to adequately test their hypothesis. Many astronomers even disagree with this hypothesis.

How likely is it that the expanding universe hypothesis is true? To answer this question, you must understand the concept of probability. Probability is simply how likely something is. A hypothesis that is very likely to be true has a high probability. One that is not likely to be proven has a low probability.

Emphasize that degree of probability is highly subjective. A phrase might be interpreted by two different people to indicate very different degrees of probability.

Statements of hypotheses often contain a **degree of probability.** The degree of probability is a word or phrase that tells the reader what the chances are that the hypothesis is true. This feature of hypothesis is important. While probability is expressed in English in many different ways, there are three words that are very useful for indicating degree of probability. They are *possible, likely,* and *probable.* **Table 7-1** shows some of the forms these words might take in a hypothesis.

TABLE 7-1 PROBABILITY WORDS IN A HYPOTHESIS

Probability Word	Form in a Hypothesis
possible	impossible, possible, possibly, possibility
likely	unlikely, likely, likelihood
probable	improbable, probable, probably, probability

You can combine these words with other words to offer a wide range of certainty (or degree of probability). **Figure 7-2** shows many of the possibilities that come from combining these words. The list ranges from the most probable at the top to the least probable at the bottom.

Section 7-4 Probability, continued

Increasing Probability →

It is highly probable that . . .
There is a strong/high probability that . . .
In all probability, . . .
It is probable that . . .
It is very likely that . . .
There is a strong likelihood that . . .
In all likelihood, . . . *Also:* . . . in all likelihood . . .
X is probably . . . *Also:* . . . probably . . .
There is a strong possibility that . . .
More than likely, . . .
It is more than likely that . . .
It is likely that . . .
It is very possible that
There is a definite possibility that . . .
It is possible that . . .
It is not impossible that . . .
It is not unlikely that . . .
It is not very probable that . . .
It is not very likely that . . .
It is unlikely that . . .

FIGURE 7-2 There are many ways to indicate degree of probability in a hypothesis. This list is only a small sampling.

We can think of probability on a sliding scale from 0 percent to 100 percent. All of our different probability words and phrases fall somewhere on that scale. The relationship between the words and numbers is not exact. For one person, probably might mean 60 percent certainty; for someone else, it could be 75 percent. When you speak or write, be very careful about your choice of probability words. Remember, very few things are 100 percent certain, and very few things are completely impossible.

0%	10–20%	20–30%	30–40%	50%	60–80%	90–99%	100%
no chance, impossible	highly unlikely, a remote possibility	a small chance	some possibility	may, might	a good chance, likely, probable	almost certain	will definitely happen

FIGURE 7-3 All probabilities fall somewhere between 0 percent, completely improbably, and 100 percent, or definite.

There are many ways to express probability in hypotheses. **Table 7-2** shows three ways of expressing a probability in a hypothesis.

Section 7-4 Probability, continued

TABLE 7-2 HOW TO EXPRESS PROBABILITY IN A HYPOTHESIS

Probability word + Hypothesis	
Probability Word	**Example**
In all probability,	In all probability, meteorites came from the broken pieces of former planets.
As far as	As far as we know, Earth is the only planet in our solar system capable of supporting life.
From what we have seen/observed,	From what we have observed, the universe will keep expanding forever.
Probability word + that + Hypothesis	
accepted	It is commonly accepted that Earth is the only planet in our solar system capable of supporting life.
chance	There is a good chance that signs of life will someday be found somewhere else in the universe.
evidence	There is some evidence that Earth is warming due to the greenhouse effect.
held	It is widely held that all the continents were once part of a single giant land mass.
indicate/suggest	Studies indicate that a periodic hole appears in the ozone layer over the South Pole.
seems/appears	It seems that Earth is undergoing dramatic changes in climate.
Hypothesis subject + Probability word + Rest of hypothesis	
expect	Considering the high amount of mercury in the water, we would expect a reduction in the fish population.
may/might/could	The dinosaurs could have been destroyed by climate changes following a meteorite collision with Earth.
thought	Galen is thought to be the father of medicine.
should	A particular reaction should occur after five minutes.

Table 7-2 can appear large and daunting. Just because a probability word is given with one of the three patterns, it does not mean that the word or phrase cannot be used with another pattern.

Section 7-4 Probability, continued

Exercise 6   Degree of Probability

Read the following hypotheses and choose an appropriate degree of probability from Figure 7-2.

a. _There is a strong probability_ that Earth and the other planets came from contracting clouds of gas.

b. _It is very possible that_ the dinosaurs were destroyed by a giant meteorite that caused a sudden climate change.

c. _It is not impossible_ that there is life on other planets.

d. _In all likelihood,_ the first inhabitants of America came from Asia.

Exercise 7   Determining Degree of Probability

Rewrite these hypotheses as statements of probability. Choose the appropriate degree of probability. Use a different probability word or phrase for each statement.

a. There is no life on the planet Mercury.

It is highly unlikely that there is life on the planet Mercury.

b. There is life somewhere else in the solar system.

There is a possibility that life exists somewhere else in the solar system.

c. That life would be different from us.

It is highly probable that any life elsewhere in the solar system would be very different from us.

d. It would be a lower form of life.

It is not impossible that it would be a lower form of life.

Section 7-4 Probability, continued

Exercise 8 **Probability Words**

Read the following passage, and pick out the words and phrases that indicate probability. List the probability words in the spaces provided. There may be more spaces than you need.

Elsewhere?

Life probably exists elsewhere. The universe is awash with places where life might have arisen. Within our solar system, Europa, a tiny moon of Jupiter is the place most likely to support extraterrestrial life. In fact, conditions there would be far less hostile to life than the conditions that are thought to have existed in Earth's primordial oceans. Our own Milky Way galaxy and the nearby Andromeda galaxy each contain more than 100 billion stars. And the universe holds more than a billion galaxies. Astronomers estimate there are 10^{20} (100,000,000,000,000,000,000) stars similar to our sun. At least 10 percent of these stars are thought to have planetary systems. If only 1 in 10,000 of these planets in the universe has the right combination of mass and distance from its sun to duplicate Earth's development, life could have arisen 10^{15} (a million billion times).

Life processes also might have arisen and evolved differently on other planets. Under different conditions, life theoretically could form from substances other than the carbon-based compounds and water that make up life on Earth. Silicon and ammonia are the most likely possibilities. Perhaps under radically different temperatures and pressures, these substances might have formed complex molecules as diverse and flexible as the carbon-based ones on Earth.

(from Biology Principles and Explorations)

probably	the most likely possibilities
might have arisen	Perhaps
most likely to support	might have formed
thought to have existed	
are thought to have	
could have arisen	
also might have arisen and evolved	
theoretically could form	

7-5 Facts, Hypotheses, and Theories

It is very important to know the difference between facts, hypotheses, and theories especially in science. Confusing something that is true with something that is unproven can you get into deep trouble. A hypothesis, as you have seen, is a guess. It is an educated guess that is based on reasonably good evidence, or facts. A **theory,** in science, is a broad generalization that explains a body of facts. The theory can explain the observed results when a hypothesis is tested. Experiments and additional evidence support the hypothesis. The theory explains these results. The difference between a hypothesis and a theory is very important. If you need help distinguishing hypothesis and theory, look at **Figure 7-4.**

Evidence can be found to dispute a hypothesis and a theory can be incorrect. Many years ago, most people had a theory that Earth was the center of the universe and that the sun revolved around Earth. Every morning they saw the sun rise in the east, move across the sky, and set in the west. These are facts based on observations. The interpretation of these facts led to the hypothesis that the sun traveled around Earth. This opinion was held for many years without any evidence to dispute it. It then became the theory accepted by most people. Later on, new methods for looking at the sky gave scientists new evidence that their old theory was false. Now we accept the theory that Earth, as well as the other planets in our solar system, revolve around the sun.

When a statement of hypothesis or theory is in the past tense, the hypothesis or theory has usually been proven incorrect. For example, in 1200, most people *believed* that Earth was the center of the universe. The verb *believed* is written in the past tense. Most people do not still believe that Earth is the center of the universe. Exercise 9 gives you extra practice using verb tense to correctly describe hypotheses and theories.

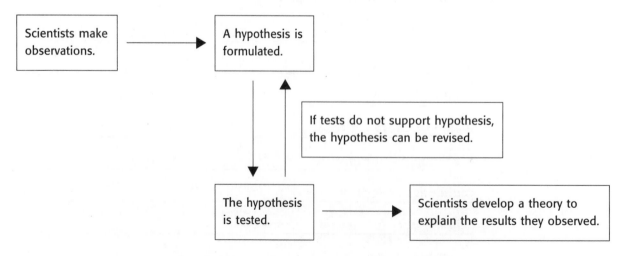

FIGURE 7-4 Theories can explain the results of an experiment.

Section 7-5 Facts, Hypotheses, and Theories, continued

| Exercise 9 | Fact versus Hypothesis versus Theory |

Put the appropriate word in the blank space. There are only five words listed below. Each word is listed in three forms. Use only one form of each word, and use each word only once.

assume	assumed	assumption
believe	believed	belief
propose	proposed	proposal
hypothesize	hypothesized	hypothesis
theorize	theorized	theory

Before 1981 no one had ever seen an atom. But the existence of atoms is not a new idea. Our understanding of atoms has been developing for more than 2,000 years.

Around 440 B.C.E., a Greek philosopher named Democritus _____**proposed**_____ that matter was made of "uncuttable" particles. He called these particles *atoms* (from the Greek word *atomos*, meaning "indivisible"). Democritus _____**assumed**_____ that all atoms were small, hard particles made of a single material formed into different shapes and sizes.

John Dalton, a British chemist and school teacher, published his own _____**hypothesis**_____ about atoms in 1803. He _____**believed**_____ that all substances are made of atoms and that atoms are small particles that cannot be created, divided, or destroyed. Atoms of the same element are exactly alike, and atoms of different elements are different.

Today, experiments have shown that the existence of protons, neutrons, and electrons inside atoms is fact. According to the current _____**theory**_____, protons and neutrons are found in the nucleus. Regions inside the atom where electrons are likely to be found are called electron clouds.

(from Holt Science and Technology: Physical Science)

Section 7-5 Facts, Hypotheses, and Theories, continued

Exercise 10 Reading for Hypotheses and Theories

Read the following passage and answer the questions that follow.

Pangaea

The passage is available on **Transparency 36.** After students have answered the questions, have them help you identify the words and phrases in the passage that indicate hypotheses. Underline these words using colored pens. Point out the steps in the development of the theory: Fact/observation leads to hypothesis. Testing of a hypothesis by gathering more evidence provides the facts that can be used to formulate a theory. Ask students how long it took for the first hypothesis to become an accepted theory.

As explorers such as Columbus and Magellan sailed the oceans of the world, they brought back information about new continents and their coastlines. Mapmakers used the information to make the first reliable world maps. As people studied the maps, they were impressed by the similarity of the continental shorelines on either side of the Atlantic Ocean. The continents looked as though they would fit together, like the parts of a giant jigsaw puzzle. Were the continents once part of the same huge landmass? If so, what caused this landmass to break apart? What caused the continents to move to their present locations? These questions eventually led to the formulation of hypotheses.

In 1912, a German scientist Alfred Wegener, proposed a hypothesis called continental drift, which stated that the continents had moved. Wegener hypothesized that the continents once formed part of a single giant landmass, which he named Pangaea, meaning "all lands."

In addition to the similarities in the coastlines of the continents, Wegener soon found other evidence to support his hypothesis. If the continents had once been joined, research should uncover fossils of the same plants and animals in areas that had been adjoining parts of Pangaea. Wegener knew that identical fossil remains had already been found in both eastern South America and western Africa. The age and type of rocks in coastal regions of widely separated areas, such as western Africa and eastern Brazil, matched closely.

Despite the evidence supporting the hypothesis of continental drift, Wegener's ideas met with strong opposition. The conclusive evidence that Wegener sought to support his hypothesis was finally discovered in 1947. As scientists examined rock samples that they brought up from the ocean floor, they made a startling discovery. None of the oceanic rocks were more than 150 million years old. The oldest continental rocks are about 4 billion years old. Here, at last, were the discoveries that Wegener had sought. They provided the scientific evidence he needed to formulate the theory of continental drift.

(from Modern Earth Science)

Name_____ Date _____ Class _____

Section 7-5 Facts, Hypotheses, and Theories, *continued*

a. What is the theory of continental drift?

The continents were once part of a single large landmass. The conti-

nents broke apart and drifted until they reached their present positions.

_____

_____

b. There are several different hypotheses in the passage. What are they?

Perhaps all the continents were once part of one great landmass. If

they had once been joined, there would be other similarities.

_____

_____

c. What are the facts and evidence for each one?

The coastlines of the continents look like they would fit together like

a giant jigsaw puzzle.

Identical fossils and rocks have been found on continents that are

now very far apart.

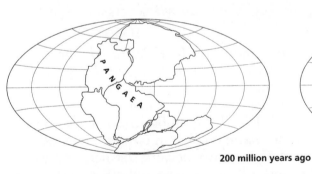

200 million years ago

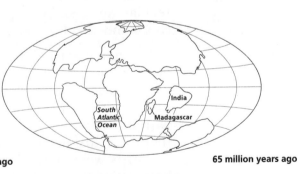

65 million years ago

135 million years ago

Present day

Continental Drift

Section 7-5 Facts, Hypotheses, and Theories, continued

The projected shape of the world 150 million years from now is available on **Transparency 37.** Use this image to review student answers to item (d). Note that this image is a prediction. Students need not match it exactly. Just make sure that students' answers are reasonable.

d. Now, study the drawings of the movement of continents over the past 200 million years and make some predictions on the position of different land masses 150 million years from now.

Central America could become shorter. North Africa might attach to
_____

Southern Europe, and the Mediterranean Sea might disappear.
_____

Australia could eventually collide with Eurasia. The region between
_____

Egypt and Turkey could disappear. Madagascar could drift further east.
_____

_____

_____

_____

_____

_____

Cause and Effect

A quick review of the topics in Chapter 5 would be an appropriate introduction to this section. Make sure students remember the concept of cause-and-effect markers.

Hypotheses predict things that will happen in the future or explain why things happen the way they do. This last function of hypotheses is often framed as a statement of cause and effect. You studied cause-and-effect statements in depth in Chapter 5. Look back at one of the hypotheses about why the dinosaurs became extinct. The dinosaurs may have been destroyed when a meteorite struck Earth and caused a sudden change in the climate. The word *caused* is a regular cause-and-effect marker. The word *when* acts as a special cause-and-effect marker.

The statement *The dinosaurs may have been destroyed when a meteorite struck Earth and caused a sudden change in the climate* actually has two hypotheses that are cause-and-effect statements. Can you identify them? The first is that the collision of a meteorite with Earth caused the destruction of the dinosaurs. The second is that the collision caused a dramatic change in climate. Because no scientists were alive when the dinosaurs became extinct, and we have little other evidence, both of these cause-and-effect statements remain hypotheses.

There are other possible explanations about what happened to the dinosaurs. Any time there is more than one possible cause of a result, a single cause must be considered a hypothesis. When all other possibilities have been disproved, the hypothesis that describes a cause-and-effect relationship can be considered a theory.

Section 7-5 Facts, Hypotheses, and Theories, continued

Exercise 11   **Cause and Effect**

Decide if each statement shows a cause-and-effect relationship. If
the statement does show cause and effect, list any cause-and-effect
markers.

a. If over time, an adaptive change within species leads to the
replacement of old species by new species, then less successful
species will become extinct.

cause and effect? (yes/no) yes_____

cause-and-effect markers: If/then_____

b. The continents will eventually rejoin and become one large landmass.

cause and effect? (yes/no) no_____

cause-and-effect markers: _____

c. Because Europa, one of Jupiter's moons, contains water, life
could have existed on Europa.

cause and effect? (yes/no) yes_____

cause-and-effect markers: because_____

d. Global warming, as a result of the greenhouse effect, may cause
melting of the polar ice caps.

cause and effect? (yes/no) yes_____

cause-and-effect markers: as a result of, may cause_____

Assumptions

Frequently, past experience and personal opinion affect how we
observe objects and events. When observations are not completely
based in fact, they include **assumptions.** For example, if you
observe a bridge over a river that appears to be sturdy, you might
consider it safe to cross. You cannot see the parts under the water
that hold the bridge up. Your observations are not complete enough
to know for certain that the bridge is safe to cross. You have made
an assumption that it is.

When you come up with a hypothesis, or a possible solution to a
problem, ask yourself how you came up with the hypothesis. Why
did you think that answer was correct? What were your assumptions? If there are several hypotheses explaining one situation,
examining how you came up with those hypotheses can help you
choose the right one. Exercises 12 and 13 will give you practice in
observing, examining assumptions, and forming hypotheses.

Name_____ Date _____ Class _____

Exercise 12   Two Trees

Observe the following drawings, and read the descriptions of where the trees grow. Compare the two trees.

Coniferous trees grow in the northern coniferous forests just below the Arctic Circle. Winters are long and extremely cold. Most precipitation falls as snow. A conifer is a tree whose seeds grow in protective cones. Most conifers do not shed their needle-shaped leaves. The leaves' narrow shape and waxy coating retain water.

(from Holt Environmental Science)

The tree above grows in the West African plains, called tropical savannas. These plains contain the greatest collection of grazing animals on Earth. Tropical savannas are found near the equator, but they get little rain. Savanna trees have large root systems. Trees and shrubs often have thorns or razor-sharp leaves.

a. Make three observations about the two trees. Use the general topics given below to make your observations.

i. shape: <u>The coniferous tree is narrow and arrow shaped. The</u>

<u>other tree has a bare trunk with a wide top.</u>

_____

ii. leaves: <u>The coniferous tree has more leaves. They are needle-</u>

<u>shaped. The other tree has sharp leaves.</u>

_____

iii. height: <u>The coniferous tree is much taller than the other tree.</u>

_____

_____

Section 7-5 Facts, Hypotheses, and Theories, continued

b. What are the reasons for the differences in the trees? Write hypotheses based on your three observations from part (a).

   i. The arrow shape of the conifer helps heavy snow fall from the tree without damaging it. The other tree is wide to allow it to collect more of the limited rainfall.

   _____

   ii. The needle-shaped leaves of the conifer help it hold moisture. The sharp leaves of the tropical savanna tree keep it from being eaten by too many animals.

   _____

   iii. The tropical savanna tree is short because it gets little water.

   _____

   _____

   _____

c. What facts about the trees can you find in the illustration and passages to support your hypotheses?

   i. Conifers are arrow shaped and live in an environment that gets a lot of snow. Tropical savanna trees live in a climate that gets little rainfall.

   _____

   ii. Conifers have waxy needles that retain water. Tropical savanna trees have razor-sharp leaves.

   _____

   _____

   iii. Conifers appear much taller than the tropical savanna trees. Tropical savanna trees get little rain.

   _____

Section 7-5 Facts, Hypotheses, and Theories, continued

d. What assumptions are your hypotheses based on?

    i. <u>Heavy snow will fall off a pointed tree. A wider tree top will</u>

        <u>collect water better.</u>

        _____

    ii. <u>Animals will not want to eat sharp leaves.</u>

        _____

        _____

    iii. <u>Lack of water produces shorter trees.</u>

        _____

        _____

Exercise 13 **Bigfoot and Littlefoot**

Study the following drawing. Then write out (a) your observations, (b) possible hypotheses about your observations, and (c) the assumptions for each hypothesis.

Name_____ Date _____ Class_____

Section 7-5 Facts, Hypotheses, and Theories, continued

a. Make observations about the picture.

   i. There are two sets of prints (tracks).

   ii. The right-hand set of prints (Bigfoot) is larger than the left-hand set. (Littlefoot).

   iii. Bigfoot's tracks are spaced farther apart as they approach Littlefoot's.

   iv. At the place where they meet, the two sets of tracks form a circle.

   v. Bigfoot's tracks continue while Littlefoot's do not.

b. Write hypotheses based on your observations from part (a).

   i. There are two animals approaching each other.

   ii. One animal is larger than the other.

   iii. Bigfoot hurried as he approached Littlefoot.

   iv. Bigfoot and Littlefoot struggle.

   v. Bigfoot eats Littlefoot and continues on his journey.

Section 7-5 Facts, Hypotheses, and Theories, continued

c. What assumptions are your hypotheses based on?

i. <u>Neither set of prints comes from an animal carrying another animal.</u>

_____

ii. <u>Larger footprints mean a larger animal.</u>

_____

iii. <u>Bigfoot hurries by lengthening his stride.</u>

_____

iv. <u>Bigfoot and Littlefoot are enemies.</u>

_____

v. <u>The only place Littlefoot could have gone was into Bigfoot.</u>

_____

GLOSSARY

assumption information that you believe is true because of your general knowledge, not because you observe it (125)

degree of probability a word or phrase that tells the reader what the chances are that a hypothesis is true (115)

evidence information to help support or reject a hypothesis (107)

hypothesis a testable statement describing why something happened or happens or describing what will happen (107)

inference a conclusion based on analysis of the data, similar to a hypothesis (109)

observation an act of recognizing or noting a fact or occurrence (109)

prediction a guess or statement about some event in the future (111)

theory a broad generalization that explains a body of facts or phenomena (120)

8-1 The Quantifying Sense

Begin this chapter with a class discussion of the relevance of using numbers in today's society. Pair students up and ask them to describe to their partner what they did last night. Tell them that they cannot use any quantifying words. They should find this task impossible, proving how important a quantifying sense is.

Whether you know it or not, you are constantly measuring, calculating, and quantifying the world around you. Even slang phrases such as *No way!* or *Awesome!* are measurements. *No way* simply means that there is a zero chance of something happening. *Awesome* means that something is really big or that it is really great in some way. Even a phrase such as *He loves her like crazy* indicates a quantity. *Like crazy* means a lot, or a great deal.

The word *quantity* probably makes you think of numbers. But quantifying is not just a matter of numbers. It is a certain sense or feel about the size, greatness, or amount of something. We can call it a **quantifying sense.** It does not have to involve numbers at all, as you can see from the examples in the last paragraph.

Even animals have a sense of quantity. Spiders tend to create a certain number of polygons when they spin their webs. And a sheep dog will know if one sheep in a large herd is missing. Whether in science or in other areas of our lives, we can better understand things if we examine them with an awareness of quantity.

In English there are many words that are used for quantifying. These words can be called **quantifiers.** Any word that represents how much, how often, how many, or how large is a quantifier. Think back to Chapter 1 in which you studied descriptions in great detail. Think about how difficult it would be to accurately describe an object without using any quantifiers. For instance, could you accurately describe a tree without saying how tall the tree is? Until now, you were probably not even aware of how often you use quantity words. Exercise 1 allows you to practice identifying quantifers.

When you think of quantity, you probably think of numbers. But quantifiers sometimes mix words with numbers. Numbers will be looked at more closely later in this chapter. For now, you should understand how numbers and words are used together. Scientific experiments often require exact measurements. Measurements are written as a number and a unit of measurement, such as 14 milliliters, 50 centimeters, or 20 milligrams. Measurements combine words (the units) with numbers (the exact quantity). Without the unit, the numbers are meaningless. Exercise 2 gives you practice combining words and numbers to quantify parts of your everyday life.

Exercise 1   Quantifiers

List all of the quantifiers in the passage found on the following page. Some of them are harder to spot than others. There may be more lines than you need.

Name_____ Date _____ Class _____

Biomes

Earth is covered by hundreds of types of ecosystems. For convenience, ecologists divide these ecosystems into a few biomes. Biomes are areas that have distinctive climates and organisms. Each biome contains many individual ecosystems. Biomes are named according to their plant life because the plants that can grow in an area determine what other organisms can live there. But what determines which plants can grow in a certain area? The main determinant is climate. Climate refers to weather conditions in an area—temperature, precipitation, humidity, and winds—over a long period of time. Temperature and precipitation (rain, sleet, and snow) are the two most important factors in a region's climate.

(from Holt Environmental Science)

When students have completed Exercise 1, place them in teams of two to review their answers. The passage is available on **Transparency 39.** Have each team come up and circle a quantifier on the overhead. Allow students to discuss the reasons for including the answers given.

hundreds	other
divide	the main
a few	a long period
distinctive	the two most important
each	
many individual	

Exercise 2   Words and Numbers

Students' answers to Exercise 2 will vary. The answers given here are examples of correct answers. Note that numerals are not the only forms of numbers that can be used.

Answer each of the following questions using a combination of words and numbers.

a. How often do you brush your teeth?

3 times a day/once or twice a day

b. How much time do you spend watching television?

20 hours a week

c. How much time do you spend on homework?

2 hours a night

d. How big is your class?

We have 24 students in our class.

Section 8-1 The Quantifying Sense, continued

Scalar Words

How often have you been asked to rate something on a scale of 1 to 10? You probably have been asked often. People like to measure things using scales. Of the many hundreds of words in the English language that can be used for quantifying, most (but not all of them) can be arranged on a scale from 0 percent to 100 percent. For example, the scale in **Figure 8-1** shows words used to explain *how often* or *how frequently* something happens. **Figure 8-2** gives another example using quantifiers that describe size.

0%	10–20%	30%–40%	50%	60–70%	80–90%	100%
never	rarely	seldom	sometimes	often	almost always	always

FIGURE 8-1 *How often* or *how frequently* something happens can range from *never* to *always*.

0%	10–20%	30%–40%	50%	60–70%	80–90%	100%
infinitely small	very small	small	medium	large	very large	the largest

FIGURE 8-2 Quantifiers to describe size can also be placed on a scale from 0 percent to 100 percent.

Ask the students what other words combine with *how* to form questions of quantity. Answers might include *how much, how many, how big, how fast,* or *how often*. In fact, answers could include *how* + any adjective.

Emphasize that the percentages in Figures 8-1 and 8-2 are not exact. Also, emphasize that two different people can interpret scalar words very differently and each can be correct.

In fact, most other groups of quantifiers can be arranged in a similar way. These quantifiers might answer questions such as *how much, how many,* or *how fast*. Another example of quantifying things along a scale can be found in Chapter 7. In the chapter on hypotheses, you studied probability, or the question of how likely something is. Figure 7-3 showed a scale of probability words similar to the scales in Figures 8-1 and 8-2.

The kinds of words that fit on a scale can be called scale words or **scalar words.** There are certain patterns of words that serve as scalars. Some of these patterns involve suffixes attached to adjectives. An example of this pattern would be the suffixes *-er* and *-est*. The adjectives big, bigg*er*, and bigg*est* are scalar words. Another pattern involves adding scalar adjectives to quantifiers. For example, the descriptive word *interesting* can be made into a scalar quantifier by adding *less* or *more* to form *less interesting* or *more interesting*. The descriptive word *big* can be made into a scalar quantifier by adding the words *very* or *not very* to form *very big* or *not very big*. If you would like a review of this concept, look back at Chapter 6.

It is important to remember that more general terms are also used for quantities. These words, such as *some, almost never,* or *approximately,* have various shades of meaning. In reading and writing science one must be aware of these different meanings.

Section 8-1 The Quantifying Sense, continued

TABLE 8-1 SCALE WORDS

	0%	10–20%	30–40%	50%	60–70%	80–90%	100%
Frequency words	never	rarely	seldom	some-times	often	almost always	always
Mass words	none	very little	not much	some	a lot of	a great deal	all
Counting words	none	very few	a few	a fair number	many, a lot of	a great many	all
Probability words	no chance	highly unlikely	some possi-bility	may	a good chance	almost certain	posi-tive, certain
Size words	infinitely small	very small	small	medium	big, large	very large	biggest, largest
Time words		very slow	slow	average (speed)	fast	very fast	the fastest

Two people can mean very different quantities when saying the same word. Just how many is *many?* How many are in a *few?* How often is *seldom?* How probable is *likely?* You might answer these questions very differently from the person sitting next to you. **Table 8-1** shows many kinds of scalar words including some general terms. You will recognize some of the words from Figures 7-3, 8-1, and 8-2.

Exercise 3 Scalar Words

The following sentences are taken from some of the reading passages in previous chapters. Use the words or forms from Table 8-1 or any other scalar words to complete the statements. The first item is done for you as an example.

a. There are a ___*large number of*___ galaxies in the universe.

b. Life ___probably___ exists elsewhere. Within our solar

system, Europa, a tiny moon of Jupiter, is the place

___most likely___ to support extraterrestrial life. In fact,

conditions there would be ___far less___ hostile to life

than the conditions that are thought to have existed in Earth's

primordial oceans.

Section 8-1 The Quantifying Sense, continued

c. The end of the Ordovician period is marked by a

_____drastic_____ change in the fossil records. A

_____large_____ portion of all life-forms suddenly disap-

peared from Earth about 440 million years ago. This extinction

was the first of five _____major_____ mass extinctions that

have occurred during the history of life on Earth. Then, about

250 million years ago, the third and _____greatest_____ of

all mass extinctions literally devastated our planet. At that time,

_____about_____ 96 percent of all animals living at that

time became extinct.

d. Plants produce oxygen. They also provide us with food;

_____almost_____ everything we eat comes from a plant or

an animal that ate a plant. And plants provide us with

_____many_____ _____other_____ useful products,

such as wood, medicines, fibers for making cloth and paper, and

rubber. Did you know that _____most of_____ the food peo-

ple eat actually comes from fruits?

Other Kinds of Quantifiers

There are other kinds of quantifying words that do not fit into the
categories discussed early in this chapter. They can be called *nonscalars*. Nonscalars come in such a variety that they cannot easily
be put into a few groups or categories. Although they are not as
common as scalar words, they are still very important quantifiers.
Most of the scalar words you have studied have been adjectives or
descriptors. Nonscalars frequently are verbs that indicate some
change in quantity. Words that suggest an approximate quantity
can also be considered nonscalars because they do not fit strictly
into a relative scale. **Table 8-2,** on the following page, gives some
examples of nonscalar quantifiers.

The nonscalar quanti-
fiers in Table 8-2 are
not all-inclusive. Ask
students to add to this
list by thinking of
other examples.
Additional entries for
the three types of
words might include
enlarge, ordinarily, and
almost.

Section 8-1 The Quantifying Sense, continued

TABLE 8-2 EXAMPLES OF NONSCALAR QUANTIFIERS

Type of word	Nonscalar quantifier	Example
Verbs that suggest a change in quantity or size	contract	When stars enter their third stage of life, they begin to contract.
	compress	We read how pressure compresses lignite, turning it into bituminous coal.
Words that indicate the normal state of things	usually	Overall, the distribution of the major biomes usually relates to climate and types of soil.
	typical	A typical flashlight has two batteries in it.
Words that suggest an approximate quantity	roughly	Over roughly 100 million years, small bodies came together to form planetesimals.
	about	The oldest continental rocks are about 4 billion years old.
	nearly	Adult amphibians eat nearly anything they can catch.

Exercise 4 **Finding the Quantifiers**

Read the following passage and list the quantifiers it contains. You may recall this passage from Chapter 2.

Cycles of the Universe

This passage is available on **Transparency 40.** Once students have completed the exercise, allow a student to use the transparency to identify the answers. Students should be able to defend their answers. Point out some of the nonscalar terms that are noted below.

contracts: to become smaller in size

swells: becomes larger

collapse: to suddenly become much smaller

We saw earlier how our sun, moon, and planets came into being. But those events are only the first stage in the life of a star. The second stage is the one our solar system is in now. This second stage lasts as long as the star, in our case the sun, has enough energy, or enough hydrogen, to keep it burning.

When hydrogen begins to run out, the star enters the third stage. At first, the star contracts; then it swells to enormous size. Some stars become giants, while others become supergiants. Giants are 10 or more times bigger than the sun. Supergiants are at least 100 times bigger than the sun.

When its atomic energy is completely gone, a star enters its final stage of evolution. Gravity causes the star to collapse inward. What is left is a hot, dense core of matter called a white dwarf. White dwarfs shine for billions of years before they cool completely.

Section 8-1 The Quantifying Sense, continued

Some white dwarfs simply cool and die. During the process of cooling, others create one or more large explosions. A white dwarf that has such an explosion is called a nova. If the star was a supergiant, the white dwarf becomes a supernova after its huge explosion.

After exploding, some supernovas contract into a tiny, incredibly dense ball of neutrons, called a neutron star. A spoonful of matter from a neutron star would weigh 100 million tons on Earth. The remains of other massive stars contract with such a force that they crush their dense core and leave what astronomers think is a hole in space, or a black hole. The gravity of a black hole is so great that not even light can escape from it.

(from Modern Earth Science)

earlier _____	**dense** _____
first stage _____	**dwarf** _____
second stage _____	**billions of years** _____
as long as _____	**cool completely** _____
enough energy or hydrogen _____	**others** _____
third stage _____	**one or more large explosions** _____
contracts _____	**huge explosion** _____
swells _____	**contract** _____
enormous size _____	**tiny, incredibly dense ball** _____
some stars _____	**spoonful** _____
giants _____	**100 million tons** _____
10 or more times bigger _____	**massive stars** _____
supergiants _____	**such a force** _____
at least 100 times bigger _____	**crush** _____
completely gone _____	**so great** _____
final stage _____	
collapse _____	
hot _____	

Name_____ Date _____ Class _____

8-2 Calculating

Students may question why mathematics is being discussed in a science book. Remind them that quite frequently mathematics is the language in which science is presented.

Calculations are often written using the symbols for basic operations: +, −, ×, and ÷. But in speaking—and frequently in writing—words must replace these symbols. If you were asked to read 1 + 1 out loud, you would say, "one plus one" without even thinking about it. **Table 8-3** lists many ways to describe mathematical calculations. Then, Exercises 5 and 6 give you practice going back and forth between words and mathematical symbols.

TABLE 8-3 TERMS FOR MATHEMATICAL CALCULATIONS

Operation	Terms	Example
Multiplication	multiplied by	x multiplied by 5 equals 27.
	the product of	The product of 12 and 5 is 60.
	by multiplying	By multiplying the two numbers, you get 74.
	times	Twelve times 5 is 60.
	twice	Twice 12 is 24.
	of	Two-thirds of 60 is 40.
	square, squared	The square of 2 is 4.
	cubic, cubed	The box has a volume of 4 meters cubed.
Addition	sum, the sum of	The sum of 30 and 12 is 42.
	plus	Thirty plus 12 is 42.
	and	Ten and 5 is 15.
	(is) added to	Thirty added to 12 is 42.
Subtraction	minus	Five minus four equals one.
	subtracted (from)	Four subtracted from five equals one.
	less	Five less four equals one.
Division	divided by	Ten divided by 2 is 5.
	by dividing	A is determined by dividing y by z.
	over	Five over 2 is 2.5.
	percent	Thirty-three-and-a-third percent of 90 is 30.
	go into	Two goes into 10 five times.
Equals	is	Eight is 15 percent of x.
	equals	x equals y.
	is determined by	x is determined by adding a and b.
	the result	The result of $2y$ plus 5 is 12.

Name _____ Date _____ Class _____

Section 8-2 Calculating, continued

Exercise 5 **Changing Words into Numbers and Formulas**

Change the following sentences to numbers and letters. The first item is done for you as an example.

a. Density (D) is defined as the amount of mass (m) in a volume (V) of one unit. In other words, the density of an object is determined by dividing its mass by its volume.

$$D = \frac{m}{V}$$

b. The result of $4x$ over 3 is 25.

$$\frac{4x}{3} = 25$$

c. Three multiplied by x is y^2.

$$3 \times x = y^2$$

d. The product of 3 and x equals 40.

$$3 \times x = 40$$

e. x raised to the third power added to 5 is 69.

$$x^3 + 5 = 69$$

f. Twelve over 4 multiplied by x results in 27.

$$\frac{12}{4} \times x = 27 \quad \text{or} \quad \frac{12}{4 \times x} = 27$$

g. Six multiplied by x is 20 plus $2y$.

$$6 \times x = 20 + 2y$$

h. x added to y is equal to z over 20.

$$x + y = \frac{z}{20}$$

i. The product of y and z is 32.

$$y \times z = 32$$

j. The value of x is determined by multiplying y by the quantity x minus 2.

$$x = y \times (x-2)$$

k. The sum of x and y is the same as y to the second power.

$$x + y = y^2$$

Note that each of these examples contains a complete sentence. Usually, mathematical sentences are complete only when they involve an equality, or some function equals a final answer. In contrast, Exercise 6 contains mathematical expressions that do not include an equal sign. The phrases corresponding to these expressions need not be complete sentences.

Make sure that students understand how the word *quantity* implies the need for parentheses in item (j).

Copyright © by Holt, Rinehart and Winston. All rights reserved.

READING SKILLS WORKSHEETS **139**

Section 8-2 Calculating, continued

l. Twice x divided by y is subtracted from z.

$z - \dfrac{2x}{y}$

m. Twice the difference of x subtracted from y is equal to 75.

$2 \times (y-x) = 75$

n. Eight is 15 percent of x.

$8 = 0.15 \times x$

o. x is determined by dividing $12k$ minus 3 by $4r$.

$x = \dfrac{12k-3}{4r}$

p. x to the third power added to 15 percent of y equals 100.

$x^3 + 0.15y = 100$

q. An area (A) of a trapezoid of bases b_1 and b_2 and height h is one half the height times the sum of b_1 and b_2.

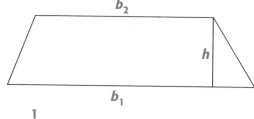

$A = \dfrac{1}{2} h \times (b_1 + b_2)$

Exercise 6   **Changing Numbers and Formulas into Words**

Now try it the other way around. Write out these symbols and formulas as words. The first item is done for you as an example. Note that some of the answers will not be complete sentences.

a. $a = \pi \times r^2$

The area of a circle equals the number pi times the radius squared.

b. $4(\sqrt{x}) - y^2$

four times the square root of x minus y squared

Section 8-2 Calculating, continued

c. $w = \dfrac{a}{a^2} + b^2 - \dfrac{b}{a^2} + b^2 m$

w equals a over a squared, plus b squared, minus b over a squared,

plus b squared times m.

d. $2(x + 6)$

two times the sum of x plus 6

_____

e. $(x^2 + 7)(y + 3)$

the quantity x squared plus 7 times the quantity y plus 3

_____

f. $9x^2 + 3 = 39$

Nine times x squared plus 3 is 39.

_____

g. $6\dfrac{x}{3}$

six times x divided by 3

_____

h. $z = \dfrac{11x + y^2}{3}$

z equals the quantity 11x plus y squared, divided by 3.

_____

i. $3x + 8 = \dfrac{28}{2}$

Three times x plus 8 equals 28 divided by 2.

_____

j. $\dfrac{5}{3}(x^2 + 2)$

five over 3 times the quantity of x squared plus 2

_____

Section 8-2 Calculating, continued

Describe Your Thinking

Scientists cannot just report a problem and suggest a solution to that problem. Good scientific reporting involves a description of how the problem was solved. This step is very important because part of making scientific discoveries is to have your findings confirmed by other scientists. To do this, one scientist must be able to read another scientist's report, follow their exact procedure, and get the same results. If other scientists do not know the correct process, they cannot confirm the findings.

When solving quantitative problems, you must describe your process using a combination of numbers and words. Exercise 6 gave you some practice describing how to solve problems. In that exercise, you were asked to convert mathematical symbols into words. By doing so, you described how to solve the mathematical expressions. In science, you will often need to describe mathematical solutions. But you will also often need to describe the solutions to nonmathematical scientific problems. Exercise 7 gives you practice describing how you arrived at particular solutions.

Exercise 7   How Did You Solve It?

While you are solving the following problems, write down the steps in your thinking. Include *all* the steps. The first item is done for you as an example.

a. If the word *sentence* contains less than nine letters and more than three vowels, circle the first vowel. Otherwise, circle the consonant that is farthest to the right in the word.

s   e   n   t   e   n (c) e

The word sentence contains eight letters. Yes, it is less than nine.

There are just three vowels, not more than three. So one of the

conditions is not met. Therefore, do not circle the first vowel.

Instead, circle the consonant farthest to the right, which is c.

b. If the circle below is taller than the square and the cross is shorter than the square, put a *K* in the circle. However, if these conditions are not true, put a *T* in the second-tallest figure. List the steps in your thought process on the next page.

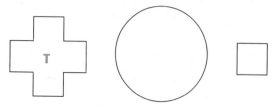

Section 8-2 Calculating, continued

The circle is taller than the square. The cross is not shorter than the square, so do not put a *K* in the circle. The cross is the second-tallest figure. A *T* is put in the cross.

_____

_____

_____

_____

_____

_____

_____

Item (c) is best done by creating a table.

	Tuesday	Wednesday	Thursday	Friday	Saturday	Sunday
	3 days before yesterday	2 days before yesterday 1 day after 3 days before yesterday	1 day before yesterday 2 days after 3 days before yesterday	yesterday	today	tomorrow

c. Tomorrow is Sunday. What day is two days after three days before yesterday?

If tomorrow is Sunday, today is Saturday. So yesterday was Friday, and the day before yesterday was Thursday. Two days before yesterday was Wednesday, and three days before yesterday was Tuesday. One day after three days before yesterday (Tuesday) was Wednesday. Therefore, two days after three days before yesterday (Tuesday) was Thursday.

_____

_____

_____

d. Decide which three numbers should come next in this series, and write a description of the pattern. Then fill in the last three numbers.

2   7   4   9   6   11   8   13 <u>10</u> <u>15</u> <u>12</u>

To get from 2 to 7, add 5. To get from 7 to 4, subtract 3. Then to get

Section 8-2 Calculating, continued

from 4 to 9, the pattern starts over by adding 5. To get from 8 to 13,

add 5. Therefore, the number after 13 should be 13 minus 3, or 10.

Then, add 5 to 10 to get 15. Then subtract 3 from 15 to get 12.

_____

_____

_____

_____

_____

e. The top four figures (1, 2, 3, and 4) have a pattern. This pattern changes in a regular (systematic) way. Try to discover the pattern and choose which item in the second group (A, B, C, or D) should occur next in the series

1 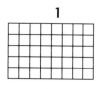 2   3 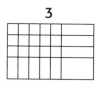 4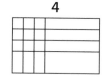

A 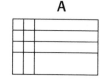 B 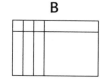 C 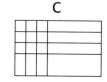 D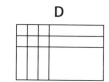

The number of vertical lines changes with each successive diagram.

The pattern is seven vertical lines, five vertical lines, five vertical

lines, then three vertical lines. The next image should have three

vertical lines. The number of horizontal lines changes with each suc-

cessive diagram. The pattern is four horizontal lines, four horizontal

lines, three horizontal lines, then three horizontal lines. The next

image should have 2 horizontal lines. Therefore, the answer is D.

_____

_____

_____

Section 8-2 Calculating, continued

Exercise 8   **What Kind of Information Is Needed?**

After reviewing the answers, ask students to develop their own incomplete questions for their classmates to figure out the missing information.

There is not enough information to solve these problems. What information do you need? Write out your answers. The first item is done for you as an example.

a. A car can travel 30 miles on a gallon of gas. How far can it go on a tank of gas?

*How much gas does the tank hold?*_____

_____

b. A bushel of apples weighs 100 pounds. If three bushels of apples weigh 300 pounds, how many apples are in three bushels?

How much does an apple weigh?_____

_____

c. Uranus has about 63 times the volume of Earth and is nearly 15 times as massive. What is the mass of Uranus?

What is the mass of Earth?_____

_____

d. Yard waste makes up nearly 1/5 of a community's municipal solid waste. Because it is biodegradable, yard waste can be allowed to decompose in a compost pile. If all yard waste became compost, how much compost would an average community produce?

How much total municipal solid waste does the average community

produce?_____

e. A molecule of ammonia contains nitrogen and hydrogen. It has a mass of 17 atomic mass units. What is the mass of hydrogen in a molecule of ammonia?

What is the proportion of hydrogen to nitrogen in ammonia?

_____

CHAPTER

NUMBERS, WORDS, AND QUANTITIES

8-3 Notation

As an additional exercise, have students play nine-square chess using the following instructions:

1. Divide the class into pairs.

2. Photocopy enough copies of the empty board on **Transparency 41** so that each pair of students has a game board.

3. Distribute one game board, three pennies, and three nickels to each group.

4. Have students lay out pieces, as shown below.

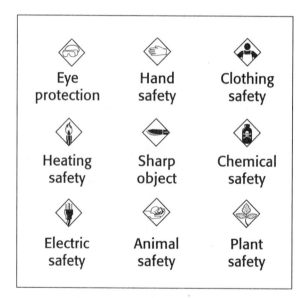

5. Explain that the pieces move as pawns do in chess. (A pawn can move only one square forward at a time. It can capture another piece only by moving into its space diagonally and taking it off the board.)

6. Explain that the winner is either the first person to get a pawn to the opposite end of the board or the last person to move.

You have probably seen coaches drawing diagrams of game strategies using *X*s and *O*s to represent players and lines to show where the players will run. This is a form of notation. **Notation** is any system of symbols. Notation can be used for scientific concepts and analysis. Notation is also used in music, dance, and games such as chess and football.

Remember how you analyzed the passages in Chapter 5 on cause and effect? You used forward and reverse arrows to show the direction of the cause and effect patterns in the sentences. These arrows are an example of notation used in a scientific analysis. **Figure 8-3** shows a common system of notation that you may find in your science textbook. Imagine how long it would take to read the instructions for an experiment if all of the safety information were written in complete sentences. The safety symbols in Figure 8-3 allow you to get the important safety information quickly.

FIGURE 8-3 Safety symbols are used to indicate the hazards in a particular scientific experiment.

Basically, there are three kinds of marks used in notation: numbers, Greek and Roman letters, and various other symbols such as ∞, $\angle$, $\geq$, $°$, $\pm$, or those found in Figure 8-3. Many of these symbols should be familiar from your math classes. There is a great deal of overlap between the symbols and letters used in math and in science. Exercise 9 will give you practice dealing with notation in scientific studies.

Section 8-3 Notation, continued

Exercise 9 **Notation in Science**

7. Ask the students what kinds of notation they should use to write down the moves of the pieces. They will need to assign labels for each square and name the pieces.

8. Have the groups play the game, and have each person record the moves of both sides. As each group finishes, have both people compare their notations. See how many different methods of notation the class comes up with.

9. As an extension, have a student that understands chess notation give a brief explanation to the class.

Point out how many different varieties of notation are used in Exercise 9: mathematical symbols, charts, pictorial representations, and letters.

In each of the following items, a notation is given. Write out an explanation for the notation.

a. the mass of Uranus > the mass of Earth

<u>Uranus has a greater mass than Earth.</u>

_____

b. Charts and graphs can also be used as notation to represent information in science.

Elemental abundance in universe

Other*
Helium
5.92%

Hydrogen
93.93%

*Oxygen 0.075%, carbon 0.047%, nitrogen 0.0094%, neon 0.0087%, magnesium 0.0042%, silicon 0.0030%, other 0.0027%

<u>The universe is made of 93.93 percent hydrogen. The universe is 5.92</u>

<u>percent helium. All other elements make up the rest of the universe.</u>

_____

c.

Eye
protection

Clothing
safety

Hand
safety

Chemical
safety

<u>The experiment requires eye, clothing, and hand protection. Chemicals</u>

<u>will be used.</u>

d. DNA, deoxyribonucleic acid, contains four nucleic acid bases: adenine (A), guanine (G), thymine (T), and uracil (U). Write out an explanation for the following notation that describes a section of a DNA strand.

AATGUTG

<u>Adenine-Adenine-Thymine-Guanine-Uracil-Thymine-Guanine</u>

Section 8-3 Notation, continued

Special Uses for Letters

The Roman alphabet is used for many types of scientific notation. If you want to find an example of a notation system in science that uses the Roman alphabet, all you need to do is look at the periodic table of the elements. The letter "H" stands for hydrogen. The letters "Fe" stand for iron. And the letters "Au" stand for gold. Another example can be found in the abbreviations for units, such as the letter "m" for meter, the letters "kg" for kilogram, and the letter "V" for volt.

Greek letters are also very common in science and engineering notation. You are probably already familiar with the letter pi, π. This letter is the factor used to find the area and circumference of a circle. Pi equals approximately 3.14159. The lowercase letters alpha (α), beta (β), and gamma (γ) are used as names for types of radiation. The letter beta is also used in the symbol β^+, which stands for the subatomic particle, the positron. The letter delta, Δ, generally symbolizes change. For example, a change in mass could be symbolized by the expression Δm. **Table 8-4** gives a list of the Greek letters that are commonly used in science. Can you think of any other Greek letters that are used for notation?

TABLE 8-4 THE GREEK ALPHABET USED IN SCIENCE

Name of letter	Upper case	Lower case
Alpha	A	α
Beta	B	β
Gamma	Γ	γ
Delta	Δ	δ
Pi	Π	π
Omega	Ω	ω

Uppercase (capitals) and lowercase (small) letters, in both the Greek and Roman alphabets may have very different meanings. For example, "G" is used as the abbreviation for gauss (a unit of electrical energy), while "g" is the abbreviation for the mass unit gram. The symbol t stands for temperature in degrees Celsius, and the symbol T stands for temperature in kelvins.

Section 8-3 Notation, continued

The use of regular or italicized type has meaning too. An italicized letter usually denotes a symbol. Most abbreviations are shown as regular type. The same letter in the same case may have different meanings depending whether the letter represents a symbol or an abbreviation. While T is the symbol for temperature in kelvins, "T" also represents the abbreviation for tesla which is an electrical unit. The lowercase letter "g" is the abbreviation for the mass unit gram, but g is the symbol for the acceleration due to gravity. You can derive the correct meaning from reading the words around the notation.

Acronyms are a special kind of abbreviation. They are usually formed from the first letters of a name. They are usually written using only capital letters. **Table 8-5** lists some common acronyms and their meanings. Can you think of any other common acronyms?

TABLE 8-5 COMMON ACRONYMS

	Acronym	Meaning
Government agencies and programs	FBI	Federal Bureau of Investigation
	CIA	Central Intelligence Agency
	NASA	National Aeronautics and Space Administration
	EPA	Environmental Protection Agency
Special systems or scientific concepts	CPR	cardiopulmonary resuscitation
	AIDS	acquired immune deficiency syndrome
	DNA	deoxyribonucleic acid
Private companies	GE	General Electric
	GNC	General Nutrition Centers
	IBM	International Business Machines
Nonprofit organizations	AFL	American Federation of Labor
	NOW	National Organization for Women
	MDA	Muscular Dystrophy Association
	WTO	World Trade Organization
Technical societies	ACS	American Chemical Society
	NSTA	National Science Teachers Association
	AMA	American Medical Association

Section 8-3 Notation, continued

Exercise 10   Special Letters

These symbols cross all subject areas of science. Students may need to use the library or Internet to research the answers. For this reason, this question might be assigned as homework.

Give a meaning for each of the following letters that are used as notation in science. Some are simple abbreviations, some are symbols, and some are acronyms. You may need to do a little research to find the answers.

a. RNA

an acronym for ribonucleic acid

b. W

watt, an abbreviation for a unit of electrical power

c. mL

milliliter, an abbreviation for a unit of volume

d. Ar

an abbreviation for the element argon

e. μm

micrometer, an abbreviation for a unit of length

f. O^+

O positive, an abbreviation for a blood type

g. λ

lambda, a symbol for wavelength

Another way to give students practice in using notation is by playing the game Battleship™, which requires students to use coordinates ("Your ship is on B7") in order to sink the enemy's ships. Students must also keep a record of the coordinates they have mentioned.

GLOSSARY

acronym a special kind of abbreviation that is usually formed from the first letters of a name (149)

notation a system of symbols used to represent something (146)

quantifier a word or phrase that indicates a quantity (131)

quantifying sense general feeling about the size, greatness, or amount of something (131)

scalar words quantifiers that can fit on a scale from 0% to 100%; terms that are a matter of degree (133)

CHAPTER

9   EXAMPLES, GENERALIZATIONS, AND ANALOGIES

9-1 Examples

Examples are an important tool in the language of science. They help you picture an idea or a concept. If you can picture or visualize an idea, that idea is much easier to understand and remember. Examples can take words that seem abstract and make them real. You will come across a lot of examples in your science books and in most other textbooks. Notice them as you read. Use them to help you understand the material and to help you remember what you have read.

Examples can also help you improve your own thinking. If something that you are reading is a little vague, try to think of an example, even if the author did not give one. If you cannot think of an example of what you are studying, you probably do not fully understand what you are reading.

Exercise 1 gives you practice identifying examples in short passages. When you are asked to pick out examples from a passage, ask yourself which part of the passage gives you a mental picture of something specific. This is a good test of which part contains the example.

Exercise 1   **Recognizing Examples**

Underline the examples in the following passages. Some passages may contain more than one example.

a. Newton reasoned that small objects fall toward Earth because they are attracted to each other by the force of gravity. But because Earth has so much more mass than a small object, <u>such as an apple</u>, only the object appears to move. Newton extended his idea to larger objects, realizing that <u>the moon is also falling toward Earth</u>. But the moon is farther away from Earth, so the effect is smaller. *(from Holt Science and Technology: Physical Science)*

b. Did you know that most of the food people eat actually comes from fruits? Fruits are the parts of a flowering plant that contain the plant's seeds. When you think of fruits, you probably think of <u>apples, oranges, and peaches</u>. However, the fruits that provide the most food to humans come from the cereal grasses. The fruits of cereal grasses, which are called grains, <u>include wheat, rice, corn, and oats</u>. *(from Holt Biology Visualizing Life)*

Section 9-1 Examples, continued

c. The matter that makes up <u>a frozen juice bar has the same iden-</u>
<u>tity whether the juice bar is frozen or has melted.</u> The matter is
just in a different form, or state. The states of matter are the
physical forms in which a substance can exist. Matter consists
of particles—<u>atoms or molecules</u>—that can move around at different speeds. The state a substance is in depends on how fast
its particles are moving. The three most familiar states of matter
are <u>solid, liquid, and gas.</u> *(from Holt Science and Technology: Earth Science)*

d. When some people think of deserts, they think of "<u>Lawrence of</u>
<u>Arabia</u>" riding a camel over towering sand dunes. Other people
might picture <u>the Sonoran desert with its mighty saguaro cac-</u>
<u>tuses, the California desert graced with Joshua trees, or the</u>
<u>magnificent rock formations of Monument Valley in Arizona and</u>
<u>Utah.</u> There are many different kinds of deserts, but the one
thing they have in common is that they are the driest places on
Earth. *(from Holt Environmental Science)*

e. All snakes are carnivores. <u>They eat small animals and eggs.</u>
Snakes swallow their prey whole. Snakes have special jaws with
five joints to allow them to open their mouth wide and swallow
very large prey. Some snakes, <u>such as pythons and boas,</u> kill
their prey by squeezing it until it suffocates. Other snakes have
poison glands and special fangs for injecting venom into their
prey. *(from Holt Science and Technology: Life Science)*

Marked and Unmarked Examples

Table 9-1 is far from complete. Ask students to think of any other words, or punctuation marks, that might be used to mark an example. Additions to the table might include *imagine* or commas that set off a parenthetical phrase.

Exercise 1 asked you to spot some examples in short passages.
Most of these examples were fairly obvious. You recognized examples by finding parts of the passage that helped you form a mental
image of something specific. Examples are not always easy to spot.
Think back to Chapter 5 on cause and effect. In that chapter, you
studied cause-and-effect markers. These markers were words or
phrases that pointed out a cause-and-effect statement. Just as there
are cause-and-effect markers, there are **example markers. Table 9-1**
lists some of the words and phrases that can indicate an example.

Occasionally, a passage will contain an unmarked example. For
this reason, it is important to develop a good sense of what an
example is. This way, you can easily identify examples even when
they are unmarked.

Section 9-1 Examples, continued

TABLE 9-1 EXAMPLE MARKERS

Word or phrase	How it is used
(As) a case in point	If you look around your classroom, you'll see that you share many physical characteristics with your classmates. As a case in point, you all have skin instead of scales.
: (sometimes a colon indicates an example)	Asbestos was widely used to reinforce cement and to make many common items: brake linings, vinyl floor tiles, residential siding, and garments to protect firefighters.
— or () (a dash or parentheses)	Acid precipitation is highly acidic precipitation (rain, sleet, or snow) that results from the burning of fossil fuels.
an example of	Gold is an example of a metal.
e.g. (*exempli gratia* or Latin for "for example")	Frogs and toads are highly adapted for life on land, e.g., adults have powerful leg muscles for jumping.
for example	For example, you may be familiar with one type of fog that results from the nightly cooling of Earth.
for instance	Ash ejected during explosive volcanic eruptions can have widespread effects. For instance, ash can blow down trees and buildings.
say	If, say, you bring water to a boil, you can kill any bacteria in the water.
such, such as	Plants provide us with many other useful products, such as wood, medicines, fibers for making cloth and paper, and rubber.
suppose	The other planets in our solar system also revolve around the sun. Suppose you were on Mercury; it would take you only 88 days to orbit the sun.
take the case of	Many scientific discoveries are accidental. Take the case of the discovery of penicillin.
to illustrate, an illustration	Neon signs can be used to illustrate how electric energy can cause gases to glow.

Section 9-1 Examples, continued

Exercise 2   **Example Markers**

The passage is available on **Transparency 43.** Review the answers with the students by underlining the marked examples on the overhead. Ask students to identify any unmarked examples. Underline these examples with a different-colored pen. The unmarked examples could include the phrase *much of your clothing is made from synthetic fibers.*

List all of the example markers found in the following passage. Some of the markers may be found in Table 9-1. Some may not. There may be more lines than you need.

You Depend on Chemicals Every Day

What is a chemical? A chemical is any substance that has a definite composition. Chemical reactions are taking place constantly all around you, and chemists are not the only people who work with chemicals. For example, a chef carefully controls the many chemical reactions necessary to produce a delicious meal.

Some people think of chemicals mainly in negative terms—as the causes of pollution, cancer, and explosions. For instance, many of these people believe that chemicals and chemical additives should be banned. But think for a moment what such a ban would mean—after all, everything around you is a chemical. Imagine going to the supermarket to buy fruits and vegetables grown without the use of any chemicals at all. The produce section would be completely empty! In fact, the entire supermarket would be empty because all foods are made of chemicals.

Without chemicals, you would have nothing to wear. Much of your clothing is made from synthetic fibers, such as polyester, that are the products of chemical reactions. Even clothing made from natural fibers, such as cotton or wool, is the product of chemical reactions.

(from Holt Chemistry Visualizing Matter)

for example	imagine
— (dash)	such as
for instance	

Functions of Examples

Perhaps without even realizing it, you have seen many functions of examples throughout this book. In Chapter 3, you learned that a complete definition needs limiting features to separate the term from all other terms in its class. These limiting features are often examples. They make the definition specific and understandable. Read the following definition of a continental ice sheet.

> A type of glacier that covers large land areas is called a continental ice sheet. For example, continental ice sheets cover most of Greenland and Antarctica.

Section 9-1 Examples, continued

The example of *continental ice sheets cover most of Greenland and Antarctica* ensures that the reader understands how large continental ice sheets are.

In Chapter 4 you studied classification. One method of classifying things is the top-down process. In this process, a general class word is accompanied by more specific class words. These specific words can be examples. For instance, metals can be classified as pure substances and alloys. Aluminum and copper are examples of pure substances. Bronze and brass are examples of alloys.

Chapter 5, on cause and effect, also used examples to illustrate its patterns. It is easy to see how examples can be used in cause-and-effect statements when you look at partial cause. Read the following sentence: *Genetics is one factor that determines what people look like.* There are many factors that contribute to a person's appearance. Genetics is only one example of these factors.

There is no pattern used in thinking or writing that cannot benefit from examples. Any time a piece of text needs to be made more clear, examples can help fill in the gaps. Exercise 3 gives you practice using examples to help explain four different images. These examples may explain cause-and-effect patterns, definitions, hypotheses, or classifications.

Exercise 3   Adding Examples

Study each image. Then write a short statement, based on the image, that uses examples to explain the image or part of the image.

a. The Life Cycle of a Star

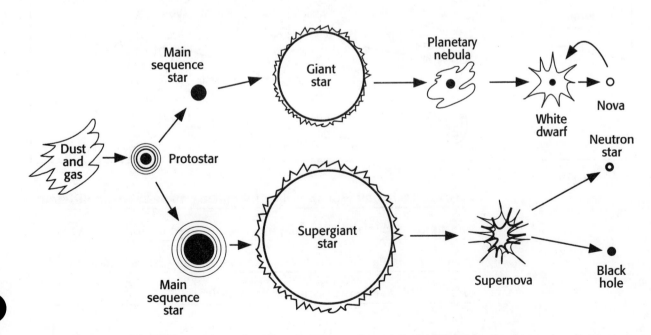

Section 9-1 Examples, continued

When dust and gas come together in the universe in just the right

way, stars can be born. There are two examples of star types that can

be born from dust and gas. These star types are giant stars and

supergiant stars.

_____

_____

_____

_____

_____

_____

_____

b. Darwin's Scientific Voyage on the H.M.S. *Beagle,* 1831-1836

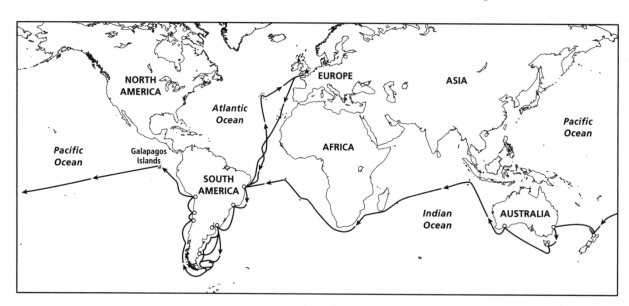

Darwin traveled all around the world making many stops on different

continents and islands. For instance, he stopped on the Galapágos

Islands in the Pacific Ocean. He also made many stops along the

eastern and western sides of South America.

_____

_____

Section 9-1 Examples, continued

_____

_____

_____

_____

_____

_____

_____

_____

c. Larger ecosystems generally support more reptile and amphibian species.

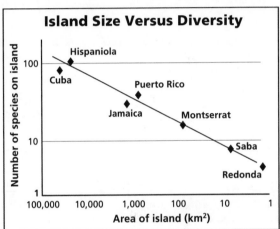

Cuba and Hispaniola are examples of relatively large Caribbean

islands. They support a wide diversity of reptile and amphibian

species. Saba, Redonda, and Montserrat are examples of relatively

small Caribbean islands. They support a smaller number of species

than the larger islands.

_____

_____

_____

_____

_____

Name_____ Date _____ Class_____

_____

_____

d. Ocean currents influence the climate of continents.

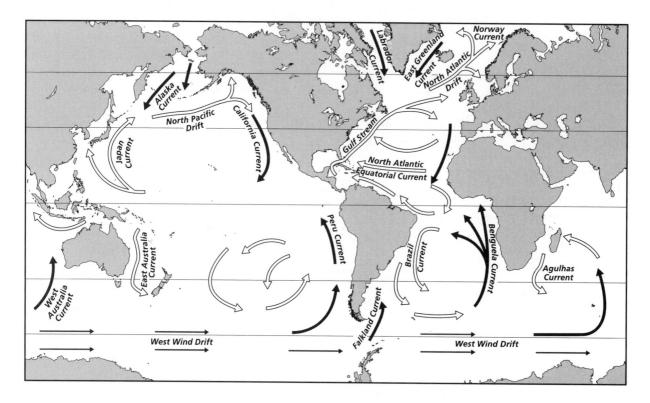

Many ocean currents flow along the coastlines of the continents. For

instance, the Gulf Stream flows along the eastern coast of North

America, and the Peru Current flows along the western coast of South

America.

_____

_____

_____

_____

_____

_____

CHAPTER

9 EXAMPLES, GENERALIZATIONS, AND ANALOGIES

9-2 Generalizations

Students may need a quick review of the material in Chapters 3 and 4 that is referred to in this section.

Think back to Chapter 3 on definitions. Terms can be defined by first assigning the term to a general class. The general class gives some information about the term but does not give any specific information. Assigning a general class to a term is a type of **generalization.** A generalization is a statement that is true but does not give complete information.

In science, it is necessary to *support* a generalization. A writer can support a generalization by using examples, details, facts and statistics, or visuals, such as pictures or charts. The generalizations in the following passage are boldface. The two sentences in the passage that are not boldface contain examples to support the generalization. The generalization and the examples together give you a complete understanding of what the biomes are.

Major biological communities that exist over wide areas on land are called biomes. The seven major biomes are tropical rain forests, savannas, deserts, temperate grasslands, deciduous forests, coniferous forests, and tundra. **Biomes differ remarkably from one another because they evolved in areas that have very different physical characteristics.** The important physical characteristics include the soils, the terrain, and the climate.

(from Biology Visualizing Life)

A generalization does not contain any details—it is not specific. For this reason, it is hard to close your eyes and picture a generalization. As you can see from the example above, it is easier to picture, or visualize, the items in the details, or the examples.

Exercise 4 **Matching Generalizations with Details**

Match the generalization (or class word) in the first column with the detail (example, or class member) in the second column.

	Generalization		Detail
a.	__6__ metal	1.	coal
b.	__4__ latitudes	2.	astronomy
c.	__5__ organ	3.	rain forest
d.	__2__ science	4.	equator
e.	__3__ ecosystem	5.	kidneys
f.	__1__ fuel	6.	aluminum
g.	__7__ synonyms	7.	speed and velocity
h.	__8__ direction	8.	clockwise

Section 9-2 Generalizations, continued

Marked and Unmarked Generalizations

Throughout this book, you have used markers to help you recognize thought patterns. However, most generalizations are *not* marked. For this reason, they can be difficult to identify. As you read, ask yourself if the information you are getting is complete. If you read a sentence and it leaves you with questions, the sentence may have contained a generalization. Sometimes, a generalization is indicated by a **generalization marker. Table 9-2** lists some words or phrases that are used to mark generalizations.

TABLE 9-2 GENERALIZATION MARKERS

Word or phrase	How it is used
generally	Animals generally need water to live.
in general	In general, precipitation is heavy where air flows upward.
by and large	By and large, most animals care for their young.
for the most part	The universe is, for the most part, made up of empty space.
generally speaking	Generally speaking, nonmetals are poor conductors.

Exercise 5   Spotting Generalizations

The passages are available on **Transparency 44.** First, review the definition of a generalization. Then read passage (a) aloud. Underline the generalization on the transparency. Ask students what questions the generalization causes them to ask. Point out that a well-written paragraph answers these questions quickly.

It may help students to realize that a generalization often appears at the beginning of a paragraph but does not have to. Also, there can be several generalizations in the same paragraph.

Underline the generalizations in the following passages. Note that some passages will contain more than one generalization.

a. By the year 2000, the world's population exceeded 6 billion. The exploding human population is placing great stress on the planet by using more energy, consuming more resources, and producing more waste than ever before.
(from Biology Visualizing Life)

b. Biology's impact on our daily lives has become so great that every person needs to know about biology in order to make many personal decisions. Perhaps its most direct effect is in medicine, whose scientific advances are improving health and health care every day. Science is exploring ways to cure inherited disorders such as cystic fibrosis and muscular dystrophy. Scientists are also searching for ways to treat and prevent AIDS.
(from Biology Visualizing Life)

Section 9-2 Generalizations, continued

   c. Power plants convert some form of energy into electric energy. Usually that form is fossil fuels. Fossil fuels—coal, oil, and natural gas—are the remains of organisms that lived millions of years ago. *(from Holt Environmental Science)*

   d. Almost all animals move around. Squirrels dash along tree branches, sharks knife through the water, and humans ride bicycles and run. However, movement is not in itself a sure sign of life. A tree does not move about, for example, but it is alive. A cloud does move about, but it is not alive. Almost all organisms respond to stimuli. Deer flee from sounds that they associate with danger, and plants grow toward light. *(from Biology Visualizing Life)*

Exercise 6 **Filling in the Details**

Provide details to support the following generalizations.

   a. Time is probably the most important way we organize our lives.

   On school days, I get up at 6:30, eat breakfast around 7, and leave

   for school at 7:30.

   b. When we observe something, we normally make assumptions.

   The first time we meet new people, we make an assumption, either

   correct or incorrect, about their personality based on how they look.

   _____

   _____

   c. One of the things we do day and night is measure, calculate, and quantify.

   Each time we pour a bowl of cereal, we measure out how much we

   think we can eat, or how much we want at the time.

   _____

   _____

Ask students to give examples from their personal lives. Select different students to recite their answers while their classmates are held accountable for the correctness of the response. It might help students to think of the given generalization as the first sentence of a paragraph. They must then write the second sentence of that paragraph to support the first.

Section 9-2 Generalizations, continued

d. Notation is a system of symbols used for all kinds of activities.

When I take notes in my classes, I cannot write down every word the

teacher says, so I use my own system of notation to jot down the

important things.

e. Classifying involves finding things that are similar and grouping them into a class or category.

In my closet, I sort my clothes using a classification pattern. Pants go

in one group, and shirts go in another.

f. We use cause-and-effect thinking to solve problems in everyday life.

When you get back a test paper with a low score, you need to ask

what caused you to do poorly on the test. This way, you can change

the outcome on your next exam.

Exercise 7 **Writing Paragraphs**

Write a one-paragraph description for each of the following images. Include a generalization and one or more supporting details.

Origin of dinosaurs and mammals	**a.**	Dinosaurs disappear at end of period	Origin of *Homo sapiens;* all recorded history
200 million years ago		**100 million years ago**	**Present**

Triassic	Jurassic	Cretaceous	Tertiary	Quaternary

Dinosaurs dominant on land; first birds

Mammals and birds become abundant; first humans appear very late in period

There were a lot of animals on Earth before humans arrived. There

were many different types of dinosaurs until they disappeared at the

_____

Section 9-2 Generalizations, continued

end of the Cretaceous period. Birds and other mammals became

abundant during the Tertiary period, but humans did not appear until

the very end of that period.

_____

_____

_____

_____

_____

_____

_____

_____

b. The shaded regions were covered with ice during the ice age.

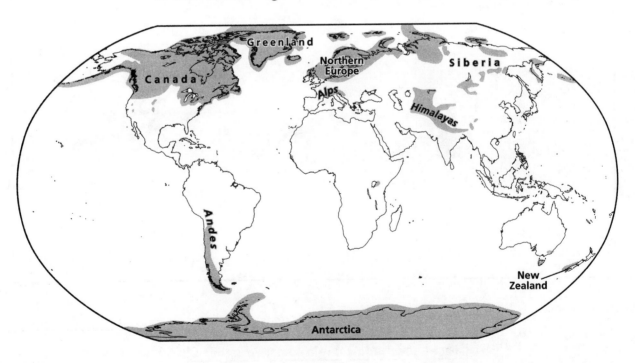

During the Ice Age, a lot of Earth was covered with great sheets of

ice. Most of Canada was covered, as was a lot of Northern Europe. All

of Greenland was under ice. Even part of the west coast of South

America was covered by sheets of ice.

Section 9-2 Generalizations, continued

_____

_____

_____

_____

_____

_____

_____

_____

_____

c. The shaded regions indicate the locations of the rain forests.

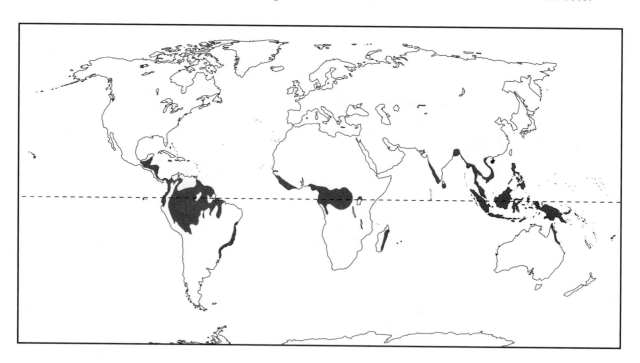

The world's tropical rain forests are located around the equator. The

best-known tropical rain forests are those in South America, but trop-

ical rain forests can also be found in central Africa. There are even

rain forests in the Pacific Islands between Asia and Australia.

_____

Section 9-2 Generalizations, continued

_____

_____

_____

_____

_____

_____

_____

_____

d. The Solar System

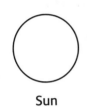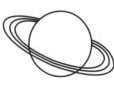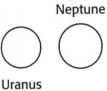

Mercury   Earth   Neptune

Venus   Mars   Pluto

Sun   Jupiter   Saturn   Uranus

Earth is not a very large planet. When compared to Jupiter and

Saturn, Earth looks tiny. Earth is only slightly smaller than Uranus and

Neptune. Earth is quite a bit larger than Mercury, Mars, or Pluto.

_____

_____

_____

_____

_____

_____

_____

CHAPTER

9 **EXAMPLES, GENERALIZATIONS, AND ANALOGIES**

9-3 Analogies

An **analogy** compares two things that seem quite different. An analogy is based on a *partial similarity*. Two things may have one feature in common, but apart from that one feature, they may be completely different. As an example, look at the following sentence.

When electrons flow consistently in one direction, as a river flows in one direction, that flow or current is called direct current.

Electricity has very little in common with a river. Electrons are much too tiny to see, so the concept of electricity can seem abstract. It is difficult to get a mental picture of electrons flowing. Giving an analogy between the flow of electrons and the flow of a river makes the concept of direct current a little easier to visualize.

Figure 9-1 gives another example of an analogy between two totally different things, a star and the human body. Keep in mind that when you are trying to create an analogy, the sky is the limit. Let your imagination run wild. All a successful analogy needs to do is help clarify a difficult concept. By using creative analogies, you may find a really original way to explain something that is confusing.

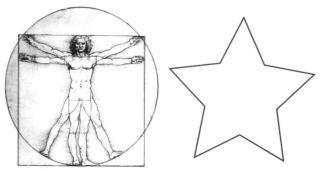

FIGURE 9-1 Are humans not made in the shape of a star?

Exercise 8   Create an Analogy

Read each phrase and try to create an analogy by completing the sentence. The first item is done for you as an example.

a. The trade winds behave like

a gentle hand that warms the land it touches.

Section 9-3 Analogies, continued

Lead the class in developing an analogy for item (b). Ask students to describe how the solar system was formed and what process they are familiar with that resembles it. Each of the phrases is based on a passage somewhere else in this text. The section numbers for each item are given below. If students need more of a context, have them refer to the original passages.

b. Section 2-3

c. Section 7-4

d. Section 3-2

e. Section 3-3

f. Section 7-4

g. Section 7-5

h. Section 9-1

i. Section 6-2

b. The formation of the solar system in some ways resembles

a bubble-gum bubble that has been blown very large and contracts

back into the center.

_____

_____

c. The chance of life elsewhere in the universe is comparable to

two people in a supermarket winding up with all of the same items in

their shopping carts.

_____

_____

d. An ecosystem is like

a city that consists of different people each doing different things,

and each having its special purpose or job.

_____

_____

e. Glaciers resemble

giant icy blankets that cover mountains and the valleys below.

_____

_____

_____

f. We can think of the number of stars in the sky as

a giant bag of jelly beans.

_____

_____

_____

Section 9-3 Analogies, continued

g. In a way, the movement of continents is analogous to

a pile of logs that breaks apart as it floats on the ocean.

_____

_____

_____

h. Life in a desert (the heat, the winds, and the dryness) is like

living inside an oven.

_____

_____

_____

i. The difference between *Homo habilis* (the earliest human form) and modern humans is like

the difference between the Wright brothers' plane and a 747.

_____

_____

_____

Marked and Unmarked Analogies

If students are having difficulty understanding how the analogy markers work, review Section 6-3 on comparison words. Analogy markers are simply a specific type of comparison word.

Just as examples and generalizations are frequently pointed out by markers, **analogy markers** often point to the use of analogies in written passages. These markers are words or phrases that relate to the analogy patterns. Because analogies are a type of comparison, you may wish to review Section 6-3. **Table 9-3** lists some of the markers used to identify an analogy. You will find that many of these markers are also listed as comparison words in Chapter 6.

Occasionally, an analogy will be unmarked. Unmarked analogies are probably one of the easiest unmarked patterns to recognize because analogies usually compare very different things. If you are reading a paragraph that discusses both leaves on a tree and fingers on a person, you would probably think the author is using an analogy. Otherwise, why would two such different items be discussed together? Exercise 9 will give you practice identifying marked and unmarked analogies in short passages.

Section 9-3 Analogies, continued

TABLE 9-3 ANALOGY MARKERS

Word or phrase	How it is used
as _____ as	If the nucleus of an atom were the size of a pinhead, the atom itself would be as big as a football stadium.
behaves like/has the same effect as	Some beneficial insects can have the same effect as pesticides: killing other insects that harm crops.
is equal to	The amount of energy saved by recycling one aluminum can is equal to the amount of energy needed to run a TV set for four hours.
acts like/is like	Polymer molecules are like giant chains whose links are atoms.
just as	Lyme disease is spread by an insect, the tick, just as bubonic plague is spread by fleas.
analogous to	Two atoms bonded together are analogous to two balls attached by a spring; they can vibrate closer together then stretch farther apart.
like/as/looks like	Ernest Rutherford believed that the electrons in an atom orbited the nucleus like the planets in the solar system orbit the sun.
may be compared to/is comparable to	A cell may be compared to a submarine. Both have a tough outer hull that seals the vessel and protects the equipment inside.
resembles	There are regions of Mars's surface that resemble dry river beds here on Earth.
We can think of _____ as a _____.	We can think of the atmosphere as a giant greenhouse that surrounds Earth.

Exercise 9   Analogy Markers

The passages in Exercise 9 are available on **Transparency 45.** You may wish to review the exercise using colored pens to underline the analogies. Other topics covered in this chapter may be reviewed using these passages as well. For instance, the second sentence of item (b) is a good example of a generalization.

Each paragraph below contains an analogy. Some analogies are marked; others may be unmarked. List any analogy markers. If the analogy is unmarked, write "unmarked" on the line.

a. In the 1980s, a new allotrope, or form, of carbon was discovered. The atoms in this allotrope form a shape like the geodesic dome designed by the innovative American philosopher and engineer Buckminster Fuller. For this reason, the 60-carbon molecule is called *buckminsterfullerene*, or, more informally, *buckyball. (from Holt Chemistry Visualizing Matter)*

like_____

b. Figuring out what the early Earth was like is similar to having a huge jigsaw puzzle with most of the pieces missing. Scientists develop ideas about what happened based on their knowledge of chemistry, biology, physics, geology, and other sciences. Astronomers are also gathering evidence from other stars where planets are forming to better understand how our own solar system formed. When new pieces of information come in, however, the pieces of the puzzle may have to be rearranged to make the new pieces fit. *(from Holt Science and Technology: Physical Science)*

is similar to _____

c. Most rocks at the surface of Earth are broken by fractures and joints. Fractures also form natural channels through which water flows. Water penetrates the rock through these channels and breaks the rock. These processes usually split the rocks into a number of smaller rock pieces. Fractures and joints increase the surface area of a rock and allow weathering to take place more rapidly.

   Picture a cube with six sides exposed. When the cube is broken once, two more surfaces are created. When each of those blocks is broken, four more surfaces are created. Splitting the original cube into eight smaller blocks doubles the total surface area available for weathering. *(from Modern Earth Science)*

unmarked _____

d. Rosalind Franklin, a chemist working at King's College in London, began studying the structure of DNA using X-ray diffraction. Franklin's X-ray diffraction images suggested that the DNA molecule resembles a tightly coiled spring, a shape called a helix. *(from Biology Visualizing Life)*

resembles _____

Functions of Analogies

Analogies are useful for explaining things that are either too large or too small to easily understand. For example, read the following description of the size of an atom. The analogy used to compare a stack of atoms with a piece of aluminum foil makes the abstract concept of a tiny atom seem much more real.

Aluminum atoms, which are average-sized atoms, have a diameter of about 0.000,000,03 cm. That's three-hundred-millionths of a centimeter. That diameter is so small that it would take a stack of 50,000 aluminum atoms to equal the thickness of a sheet of aluminum foil from your kitchen!

(from Holt Science and Technology)

Section 9-3 Analogies, continued

Just as analogies can help a reader understand the size of something very small, they can also help a reader understand the size of something very large. Examine the following passage describing the size of a giant landfill.

What is the largest structure ever made by humans? It's not the Great Wall of China that extends across northern China for 6300 km. It is the Fresh Kills landfill on Staten Island, New York. If the amount of trash the landfill holds were spread over 1000 football fields, the mound would be as tall as a 21-story building.

(from Holt Chemistry Visualizing Matter)

Analogies have the same functions as examples. They persuade. They help define a concept. They present an abstract idea in a concrete way to help you understand it better. In the following analogy, the author is explaining the abstract concept of matter being made up of a combination of different atoms. Also notice the example that can be found in the passage—*desks, chalk, paper, and even your friends.*

Have you ever stopped to consider that by using just the 26 letters of the alphabet, you make all of the words you use every day? Even though the number of letters is limited, their ability to be combined in different ways allows you to make an enormous number of words.

Now look around the room. Everything around you—desks, chalk, paper, and even your friends—is made of atoms of elements. How can so many substances be formed from about 100 elements? In the same way that words can be formed by combining letters, different substances can be formed by combining atoms.

(from Holt Science and Technology: Physical Science)

Because analogies usually relate things that cannot be seen with ordinary items that you can see (such as the letters of the alphabet), they also help the reader to remember the information.

Exercise 10   Analogies and Similarities

Read the passage and complete the table that follows it. As you read, think about what the passage is trying to tell you. Then identify the analogies and determine what makes the two things similar.

Plant Systems

Did you know that you have something in common with plants? You have different body systems that carry out a variety of functions. For example, your cardiovascular system transports materials throughout

_____

Section 9-3 Analogies, continued

_____

your body, and your skeletal system provides support and protection. Similarly, plants have systems too—a root system, a shoot system, and a reproductive system.

A plant's root system and shoot system supply the plant with needed resources that are found underground and above ground. The root system is made up of roots. The shoot system is made up of stems that bear leaves, cones, flowers, and fruits.

Roots supply plants with water and dissolved minerals. Roots support and anchor plants. Like the outermost layer of cells in your skin, the layer of cells that covers the surface of roots is called the epidermis. Some cells of the epidermis extend out from the root. These cells, which are called *root hairs,* increase the amount of surface area through which roots can absorb water and minerals.

The blank table is available on **Transparency 46.** When this exercise is finished, select a student to moderate the completion of the table on the overhead projector.

A stem connects a plant's roots to its leaves. Stems support the plant body just as your skeleton supports your body. Stems transport materials between the root system and the shoot system. Some stems store materials.

(from Holt Science and Technology: Life Science)

Item	Similarity (analogy)	Reason for similarity
Root system and shoot system	cardiovascular system, and skeletal system	transport nutrients through body or plant, and provide support
Roots	skin	outermost layer called epidermis, have hairs attached
Stems	skeletons	both provide support and structure

GLOSSARY

analogy a comparison based on a resemblance between two things that are otherwise different (166)

analogy marker a word or phrase that indicates an analogy (168)

example marker a word or phrase that indicates an example (152)

generalization a vague or incomplete statement (159)

generalization marker a word or phrase that indicates a generalization (160)

CHAPTER

10 **SUMMARY AND REVIEW**

10-1 Analyzing Text

Begin with a review of the main ideas of Chapters 1 through 9. Place each chapter title, in turn, on the board or transparency, and ask students to identify and describe the thought patterns that were highlighted in that chapter.

You have now examined nine different skills or thought patterns that will help you successfully read and understand your science (or any other subject) textbooks. You need to see how these patterns work together to help you understand the scientific way of thinking. In this final chapter, you will examine how these different skills fit together to support or reinforce one another. You will also work on developing your ability to use these different thought patterns in your writing.

Table 10-1 shows the different patterns used by writers of science texts. You have seen these patterns separately in Chapters 1 through 9. Throughout this text, you have been asked to look at different passages, and identify one of these patterns in that passage. But passages in a textbook, or any other book for that matter, will not simply contain one of these patterns. They will contain many of them. In fact, the passages that you have already seen throughout this book have actually had multiple patterns in each passage. You were asked to look for only one pattern at a time.

The passage in Exercise 1 first appeared in Chapter 3. You were asked to study it for patterns involved in defining terms. Now you will be asked to look at the passage again and find all of the different patterns it contains. One of the ways you learned to identify different patterns was by looking for markers, or words and phrases that pointed out specific thought patterns. Exercise 2 gives you practice looking for many different types of markers in a single passage. To complete these exercises, you may need to turn back to the previous chapters in this text. The tables containing the different pattern markers in those chapters will also be helpful.

TABLE 10-1 THOUGHT PATTERNS

Thought Patterns		
spatial order	classifying	hypotheses
time order	cause and effect	quantifying
defining	comparison	examples

Exercise 1 **Finding Thought Patterns**

Read the passage on the following page and pick out the different thought patterns you have studied. Simply write down the kind of thought pattern or patterns (there may be more than one) in the lettered sentences. The first item is done for you as an example.

Section 10-1 Analyzing Text, continued

Fog

[a] Fog, like clouds, is the result of the condensation of water vapor in the air. [b] The chief difference between fog and clouds is that fog forms very near the surface of Earth when air close to the ground is cooled. [c] For example, you may be familiar with one type of fog that results from the nightly cooling of Earth. This type of fog is called *ground fog.* Ground fog usually forms on calm, clear nights. [d] It is thickest in valleys and low-lying places because the dense, cold air in which it forms sinks to the lower elevations.

Two other types of fog often form inland. [e] An *upslope fog* is formed by the lifting and cooling of air as it rises along land slopes. Upslope fog is really a kind of cloud formation at ground level. [f] A type of fog known as *steam fog* usually forms over inland rivers and lakes. Steam fog is a shallow layer of fog formed when cool air moves over a warm body of water.

(from Modern Earth Science)

a. _comparison, cause and effect_

b. _comparison, cause and effect_

c. _example_

d. _cause and effect, spatial order_

e. _informal definition, cause and effect_

f. _classification, probability_

Exercise 2   Markers

Determine which words in the lettered sentences are markers for the given pattern. If a pattern is unmarked, simply write "unmarked" on the line provided.

Pangaea

[a] As explorers such as Columbus and Magellan sailed the oceans of the world, they brought back information about new continents and their coastlines. Mapmakers used the information to make the first reliable world maps. [b] As people studied the maps, they were impressed by the similarity of the continental shorelines on either side of the Atlantic Ocean. [c] The continents looked as though they would fit together, like the parts of a giant jigsaw puzzle. [d] Were the

Section 10-1 Analyzing Text, continued

continents once part of the same huge landmass? If so, what caused this landmass to break apart? What caused the continents to move to their present locations? These questions eventually led to the formulation of hypotheses.

e In 1912, a German scientist Alfred Wegener, proposed a hypothesis called continental drift, which stated that the continents had moved. f Wegener hypothesized that the continents once formed part of a single giant landmass, which he named Pangaea, which means "all lands."

g In addition to the similarities in the coastlines of the continents, Wegener soon found other evidence to support his hypothesis. h If the continents had once been joined, research should uncover fossils of the same plants and animals in areas that had been adjoining parts of Pangaea. i Wegener knew that identical fossil remains had already been found in both eastern South America and western Africa. The age and type of rocks in coastal regions of widely separated areas, such as western Africa and eastern Brazil, matched closely.

(from Modern Earth Science)

a. cause and effect   as _____

b. comparison   similarity _____

c. analogy   like _____

d. hypothesis   unmarked _____

   time   once _____

e. time   in 1912 _____

   hypothesis   proposed _____

   informal definition   which _____

f. hypothesis   hypothesized _____

   time   once _____

g. comparison   similarities _____

   time   soon _____

h. cause and effect   if. . . should _____

i. comparison   identical, both _____

Section 10-1 Analyzing Text, continued

Exercise 3   Patterns and Markers

This exercise is intended to merge what students have learned through Exercises 1 and 2. The original passage can be found in Section 8-1. The passage is available on **Transparency 39.** The blank lines are available on **Transparency 48.** Select students to help you fill in the blanks as you review the answers using the overhead.

List the thought patterns found in the sentences below, as you did in Exercise 1. Then list any markers that indicate those thought patterns, as you did in Exercise 2. If a pattern is unmarked, simply write "unmarked" on the line provided.

Biomes

[a] Earth is covered by hundreds of types of ecosystems. [b] For convenience, ecologists divide these into a few biomes. [c] Biomes are areas that have distinctive climates and organisms. [d] Each biome contains many individual ecosystems. [e] Biomes are named according to their plant life because the plants that can grow in an area determine what other organisms can live there. But what determines which plants can grow in a certain area? [f] The main determinant is climate. [g] Climate refers to weather conditions in an area—temperature, precipitation, humidity, and winds—over a long period of time. [h] Temperature and precipitation (rain, sleet, and snow) are the two most important factors in a region's climate.

(from Holt Environmental Science)

	Thought pattern	**Marker**
a.	*quantifier*	*hundreds*
	classification	*types*
b.	classification	divide
	quantifier	a few
c.	formal definition	unmarked
	example	that have
d.	quantifier	each, many
e.	cause and effect	because, determine
f.	probability	main
g.	example	— (dash)
	time	over a long period of time
h.	example	parentheses
	quantifier	two most important

CHAPTER

10 SUMMARY AND REVIEW

10-2 Fitting Patterns Together

The passage, "Glaciers" is available on **Transparency 13.** Select a student to read the passage while other students are chosen to signal when the sentences that define a glacier, classify the various types of glaciers, compare glaciers, and give examples are read. Point out the **spatial relationships** (long, narrow, high mountainous, and large), the **quantifiers** (two main types and millions of square kilometers), and the **comparison markers** (distinguished by and the other type).

Identifying different thought patterns is very important, but without knowing how they work together to support each other, the identifications are useless. The best way to study how patterns work together is to look at a sample passage. Take another look at this passage on glaciers, from Chapter 3. It starts off with a **formal definition** of a glacier. It **classifies** two types of glaciers and **compares** them to each other. It then gives an **example** of where each type of glacier can be found.

Glaciers

Glaciers are masses of moving ice. There are two main types of glaciers; they are distinguished by their size and where they are formed. One type of glacier is formed in mountainous areas. As the ice moves down a valley, it produces a *valley glacier*, which is a long, narrow, wedge-shaped mass of ice. Valley glaciers are best developed in the high mountainous regions of the world, such as in coastal Alaska, the Himalayas, the Andes, the Alps, and New Zealand.

The other type of glacier covers large land areas. These masses of ice, called *continental ice sheets*, occupy millions of square kilometers. Today, continental ice sheets are found only in Greenland and Antarctica.

(from Modern Earth Science)

Exercises 4, 5, and 6 ask you to analyze three different passages to see how they are built from different thought patterns. The thought patterns work together to tell a complete story, just as the patterns did in the passage on glaciers. The following passage is also one you have seen before. It first appeared in Chapter 4. Below the passage, you will find a step-by-step analysis of the patterns in the passage.

On the Rocks

The passage, "On the Rocks" is available on **Transparency 22.** Use this passage to model a good analysis by a step-by-step dialogue reviewing the analysis. Go slowly to allow students to focus on the process.

Geologists study the forces and processes that act upon the rocks of Earth's crust. Based on these studies, geologists have classified rocks into three major types: igneous, sedimentary, and metamorphic. The classification is based on the way the rocks are formed. Igneous rock forms when magma cools and hardens. Magma is called *lava* if it cools at Earth's surface. Sedimentary rock is formed when fragments of rock, minerals, and organic matter harden after being compressed and cemented together. The word *metamorphic* means "changed

Section 10-2 Fitting Patterns Together, continued

form." Metamorphic rocks come from other rocks that are changed by certain forces and processes, including tremendous pressure, extreme heat, and chemical processes. Any of the three major types of rock can be changed into another type.

(from Modern Earth Science)

1. The passage is about rocks: the different kinds of rocks and how they are formed.
2. It starts off by **classifying** the rocks into three types.
3. It then gives the basis for the **classification**—the way rocks are formed.
4. At the same time, it is **comparing** the different types of rocks. There are no comparison words stating that it is a comparison. In other words, the comparison is **implied** but not **stated** (it is **implicit,** not **explicit**).
5. The different origins or causes also provide **informal definitions** for the different types of rocks. For example, the passage tells you that igneous rock forms when magma cools and hardens. This **cause-and-effect** pattern serves to define what igneous rock is, and to separate it (or **compare** it) from sedimentary and metamorphic rock.

Exercise 4   Analyzing for Patterns

Exercise 4 could be done in small groups so that students can help each other with the analysis. When the exercise is completed, select a team to present its analysis using the passage on **Transparency 49** while another team is selected to provide a critique.

Using the lines below, analyze the following passage the same way that "On the Rocks" was analyzed for you.

Fossils and Evolution

According to biologists, all organisms living today evolved from earlier, simpler life-forms. The modern horse, for example, evolved from an ancestor that existed 50 million years ago. The earlier relative was the size of a dog and had four toes on its front foot, compared to its modern version, which has only one.

Animals with backbones are called vertebrates. Penguins, alligators, bats, and humans all have backbones and are thus considered vertebrates. The front limbs (known as forelimbs) of all these vertebrates have similar sets of bones. The functions of these structures have evolved into different uses. And yet, the similarity in the structure of these bones can still be seen, suggesting that all vertebrates share a common ancestor.

(from Biology Principles and Explorations)

The passage is about how fossils have led to the idea of evolution. The

passage starts off by combining an **example** of evolution and **compari-**

Section 10-2 Fitting Patterns Together, continued

son: comparing modern and earlier horses. It also compares the early

horse to a dog. The comparison uses quantifiers including size and num-

ber of toes. The passage then gives an informal definition of a verte-

brate. It also provides examples of vertebrates as part of the informal

definition. The passage gives an informal definition of forelimbs. It then

uses forelimbs as a basis of comparison for the examples that it just

mentioned. Finally, the passage gives a hypothesis, marked by the word

suggesting, that all vertebrates share a common ancestor.

_____

_____

_____

_____

_____

Exercise 5   More Practice with Analyzing

Analyze the following passage in the same way that you analyzed
the passage in Exercise 4.

If students completed
Exercise 4 in small
groups, allow them to
work individually on
this exercise using
what they learned
from Exercise 4.

Weathering and Erosion

One result of weathering is the formation of regolith, the layer of
weathered rock fragments covering much of Earth's surface. Beneath
the regolith lies the solid, unweathered rock that we call bedrock.
Eventually the uppermost rock fragments weather and form a layer of
very fine particles. This layer of small rock particles becomes soil. Soil
is a complex mixture of minerals, water, gases, and the remains of
dead organisms. As plants and animals die, their remains decay and
produce humus, a dark organic material that enriches the soil.
(from Modern Earth Science)

The passage discusses how weathering produces the different levels of

rock and soil on Earth's surface. The passage starts by using a cause-

and-effect pattern to give an informal definition of the term *regolith.*

Section 10-2 Fitting Patterns Together, continued

Then the passage uses **spatial order** to help **define** the term *bedrock.* A

time word (eventually) is used as part of a **cause-and-effect** pattern

(fragments form or cause fine particles). **Spatial order** also contributes to

this description (uppermost). A **time word** and a **generalization** with

examples help **define** the term *soil.* A **cause-and-effect** pattern adds to

the **informal definition** of the term *humus.*

_____

_____

_____

_____

_____

Exercise 6 **Interacting Thought Patterns**

The passage is available on **Transparency 25.** The passage originally appeared in Section 4-4. There is also an implied classification in the passage. The passage has classified forests into three types.

Read the following passage and answer the questions that follow.

Forests

How do forest ecosystems differ? One way is in their location. Tropical rain forests are located in a belt around Earth near the equator. In contrast, deciduous forests generally occur between 30° and 50° north latitude, while coniferous forests, or taiga, stretch in a broad band across the Northern Hemisphere just below the Arctic Circle. As a result, tropical rain forests are always humid and wet, whereas deciduous regions can have extreme seasonal variations. In deciduous regions, summer temperatures can soar to 35°C (95°F), and winter temperatures often plummet well below freezing. Coniferous forests have short, cool summers and long, cold winters. Average subfreezing temperatures often plummet to -20°C (–4°F).

Coniferous forests also get very little precipitation (20–60 cm or 9–27 inches), most of which falls as snow. Deciduous forests are moist and receive 75–250 cm (34–114 in.) of precipitation annually. The tropical rain forests get about 250 cm (114 in.) of rain a year.

The rain and snow in a deciduous forest aid in the decomposition of fallen leaves and make the soil rich and deep. Conifer needles contain acidic substances, and when they die and fall, they acidify the soil. As a result, the soil of coniferous forests is less fertile. Rapid

Section 10-2 Fitting Patterns Together, continued

decay in tropical rain forests returns nutrients to the soil, but these nutrients are washed away by rainfall, so the soil is usually thin and poor. Still, the rain forest has the greatest variety of plants and animals of any region of the world. Deciduous forests have a wide variety of plants and animals, but not nearly as many as tropical rain forests have. Most plants cannot grow in acidic soil, which is one reason that coniferous forests have a limited variety of plants.

(from Holt Biology Visualizing Life)

a. What are the two main thought patterns in the following passage?

comparison and cause and effect

b. Give three examples of how these two thought patterns interact in the passage.

   i. A comparison of the three types of forests is based on the climate in each type. The passage states that the climates are a result of (cause and effect) location.

   ii. The forests are also compared based on precipitation and quality of soil. The quality of soil is partly affected (cause and effect) by the amount and type of precipitation.

   iii. The final comparison is based on the variety of plant and animal life in each type of forest. This variety is affected by the quality of soil.

CHAPTER

(10) SUMMARY AND REVIEW

10-3 Using Thought Patterns in Your Writing

You have now learned how the nine different thought patterns can work together. You have looked at some examples covering many different topics. You have even taken these examples apart to see how they are put together. But do you really understand how to integrate these thought patterns? The best test of whether you fully understand a concept is to try to put the concept to use.

The following exercises will lead you through a process to help you improve your own writing. Throughout your practice, you may wish to review the first nine chapters of this book. You will need to be familiar with many types of markers so that you can successfully include them in your writing. Try to be as creative as possible. Use as many thought patterns and different markers as you can.

Exercise 7   Fill In the Markers

Students' answers will vary. The answers given here are the answers from the original passage, which can be found in Section 5-2. Allow students to check their responses with the passage from Chapter 5 after they have completed the exercise. The passage, including the blank lines, is available on **Transparency 50**. The complete passage is also available on **Transparency 30**.

Fill in the blanks. The kind of marker you will need is indicated in parentheses. The first item is done for you as an example.

A Star Is Born

A star begins as a nebula, a cloud of gas and dust. The particles in a nebula are held together loosely. When an explosion from a nearby star puts force on the nebula, **(quantifier)** _____*some*_____ of the particles are compressed, and the nebula begins to contract.

Gravity **(cause and effect)** _____causes_____ the nebula to continue to shrink. As the nebula becomes smaller, it begins to spin more rapidly. You may have seen the effect of decreasing diameter on the speed of a spinning object, **(example)** _____such as_____ an ice skater. The rate of spin increases as a spinning skater pulls his or her arms in closer to the body.

The shrinking, spinning nebula begins to flatten into a disk of matter with a central core called a protostar. That protostar begins to heat up **(cause and effect)** _____as a result of_____ two factors. **(example)** _____One factor_____ is collision. **(cause and effect)**

Section 10-3 Using Thought Patterns in Your Writing, continued

_____As_____ the particles move together, they collide and

produce heat energy. **(example)** _____The other factor_____ is pressure.

As the nebula shrinks and the force of gravity pulls matter toward its

center, the pressure in the core increases. All materials become

warmer when compressed.

(from Modern Earth Science)

Exercise 8 **What Kind of Marker Is It?**

This passage originally appeared in Section 2-3. The passage, without the markers noted, is available on **Transparency 9.** You may wish to use different-colored pens to highlight the different types of markers on the overhead as a review of the exercise.

Using Exercise 7 as a model, list the type of marker in the spaces
provided. The marker will follow the space for its type.

Formation of the Solar System

(_____quantifier_____) About 4 billion to 5 billion

(_____time_____) years ago, shock waves from a supernova

(a (_____quantifier_____) giant exploding star) or some other force

(_____cause and effect_____) caused a cloud of dust and gas to contract.

The cloud of dust and gas that formed our solar system over time is

called the solar nebula. (_____cause and effect_____) When the tempera-

ture at the center of the nebula became hot enough, hydrogen fusion

began and the sun was formed. About 99 percent of the matter in

the solar nebula became part of the sun.

During a period of roughly 100 million years, the small bodies of

matter in the solar nebula came together to form what are called

planetesimals. (_____cause and effect_____) Through collisions and the

force of gravity, some of these planetesimals gradually joined to form

much larger bodies called protoplanets. (_____time_____)

Eventually, the protoplanets condensed into our existing moons and

planets.

(from Modern Earth Science)

Section 10-3 Using Thought Patterns in Your Writing, continued

Exercise 9 **Define, Categorize, and Give Examples**

Exercise 9 could be assigned as homework to give students ample time for creative answers. You might wish to alter this exercise so that students are required to write paragraphs on some subject they are currently studying in their science class.

Choose one of your favorite topics and write one or two paragraphs on it. Define it, divide it into different categories, and give some examples of items in the different categories. For instance, if your topic is music, what are some of the different types of music?

_____

_____

_____

_____

_____

_____

_____

_____

_____

_____

_____

_____

_____

_____

_____

_____

_____

Section 10-3 Using Thought Patterns in Your Writing, continued

Exercise 10 **Using Thought Patterns**

Exercise 10 could be assigned as homework to give students ample time for creative answers. Make sure students use at least three of the thought patterns they have learned. Students should be encouraged to use as many different patterns as possible.

Write a short essay on animals. Choose any aspect that you like. Try using several different thought patterns in your writing. You must use at least three thought patterns, but use as many as possible.

_____

_____

_____

_____

_____

_____

_____

_____

_____

_____

_____

_____

_____

_____

_____

_____

_____

_____

_____

_____

_____

Exercise 9 Terms Frequently Used in Descriptions

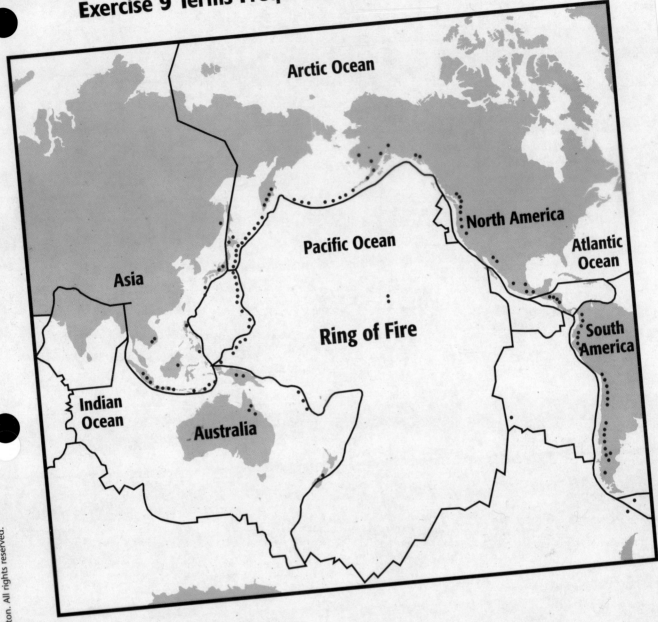

Arctic Ocean

Pacific Ocean

North America

Atlantic Ocean

Asia

Ring of Fire

South America

Indian Ocean

Australia

Exercise 1 Time Markers

Life Begins

The earliest traces of life are found as tiny fossils in 3.5-billion-year-old rocks from the ancient seas. Earth's first cells were bacteria. Unlike the interior of today's plant and animal cells, the insides of these early forms were like a warehouse—an open space within which all of the contents of a cell were free to move about. For over a billion years, bacteria were the only living things on Earth.

Then, about 1.5 billion years ago, a new kind of organism called the protist, evolved. Most protists are single-celled organisms. The next stage is the appearance of multicellular organisms. The first known fossils of multicellular organisms were found in 630-million-year-old rocks from southern Australia.

All the major groups of organisms that survive today, except plants, originated sometime during the first hundred million years of this period, which is called the Cambrian period. The Cambrian period lasted from just less than 600 million years ago to about 500 million years ago. Life was more diverse in the Cambrian seas than it has ever been since.